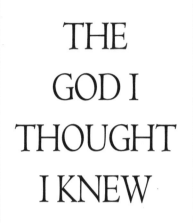

THE
GOD I
THOUGHT
I KNEW

THE GOD I THOUGHT I KNEW

*My Experiences
Growing Up Catholic*

MICHAEL R. TALAGA

NORTHFIELD PUBLISHING
CHICAGO

ISBN: 1-881273-82-2

1 3 5 7 9 10 8 6 4 2

Printed in the United States of America

I dedicate this book to Noreen,
my beautiful wife of my youth,
the one who loved me as Christ did.
By the grace of God,
through the might and steadfastness of prayer,
my wife helped to put my hand
on the door that led to life.
I am forever grateful to my Lord
for the work that He did through her love and faith.

CONTENTS

INTRODUCTION

This book was written out of self-reflection. I want to give the reader a true story about transformation, a transformation that did not come out of self, but rather from outside of myself. This book was not written for the academic world, nor was it written against anyone. Rather, I hope it shows a real-life perspective by a person whose very life has undergone a dramatic change.

Being raised a Roman Catholic, I was taught many things about God and the Catholic Church. I not only experienced these things in my parochial elementary school environment, but in my family and in my community. We were Catholic through and through. We studied under the teachings of devoted nuns who belonged to the order of the Sisters of Nazareth. Back in the days when all nuns dressed in their full habits, these dedicated women developed and shaped our belief in God.

The teachings were clear to me. For the first hour of each day, more than fifty students in my class, almost all of Polish heritage, studied the Catholic religion for eight years steady. These were our molding and shaping years.

We were like small sponges soaking up the religious teachings of the Church. The teachings were systematic and universal. We learned about such things as the Trinity, the Ten Commandments, sins (both mortal and venial), the Virgin Mary, the Pope, the Cross, the Resurrection, Saint Peter and Saint Paul, the seven sacraments, the Mass, Heaven, Hell, Purgatory, and someplace called Limbo. We learned all the foundations. There were the seven sacraments of baptism, penance, communion, confirmation, marriage, ordination, and extreme unction. These were the heart and core of my religious beliefs. These tenets and precepts were my foundation; this was my way of life and the beginning of my understanding of God and His kingdom.

If our purpose or quest in life is to come to know God, then we need to experience Him, not just know about Him. I can't experience Him for you; you must know Him personally. Only God can make this possible.

My hope is to draw you a picture using words, verbal sketches if you will. And although these verbal sketches will never portray the wonderful glory and majesty of God Himself, they can provide a glimpse of what He and His kingdom are like. This book may bring back a flood of memories of the earlier days of your religious instruction. I pray that this book will bring you to an understanding of yourself but most importantly, of God Himself, through His Son, Jesus.

I pray with all my heart that each person I may engage with this book might find what I have found. May you come to know the Peace that is beyond all understanding. Let's begin.

Chapter One

WHAT TIME
IS IT?

It seems like only yesterday that my daughter, Erin, was making her way out the front door of our house to attend her first day of school in the first grade. My wife, Noreen, and I had endeavored to prepare her to attend school. She had attended a preschool for tots that helped the kids understand the workings of a school day. The teachers taught the children social skills, including what it means to interact within a group of students and how to share things with one another. They learned the concept of letters that make words and numbers that communicate measurements. The very basics of getting along in life were brought to their attention in a school-like setting in a systematic fashion.

After preschool came a year of kindergarten—another nine months of getting ready to enter the next twelve to sixteen years of a formal education. And all of this to get my daughter ready for the next forty to forty-five years of life. We spend much time in getting ready for our future.

Some of us wish we could go back in time in order to

relive our lives differently. Based on our knowledge now, we wish we had the ability to transcend time and relive the time that we had. Some of us wish we could speed up time to enter a point in the future. Maybe it will be that job promotion that was promised to us—"in the near future." Maybe it's a fast-forwarding to the end of the ninth month of a miserable pregnancy, so that we can enjoy the exhilaration of birth and get the days of discomfort behind us quickly. Most of us are not content with living in time; we wish we had the power to make it our slave, rather than the other way around. But, fortunately, none of us has the knowledge or power to manipulate time. We live in it and by it. It is a level playing field, and we all live by the same clock. We are all in the same quarter of the game.

When I look at my daughter Erin, who is now twenty-one years old, I see the likeness of my wife, Noreen. I see my wife's smile; I see her bright blue eyes. I also remember my little redheaded, ponytailed girl going out the door, hurrying to her first day of elementary school. The only thing that separates this vision is time. Whether I see her as she is today or remember her as she was then, I see a vibrant young woman distinctly fashioned by God for Himself. I see a young woman whose laughter comes easily and who is the joy of her father's heart. I see her as an opportunity for God to reveal His glory, His workmanship. I think of God when I think of my daughter. It begs me to ask the question: *Why did God make her?*

The answer to this profound question can be found in the Catholic catechism that I studied more than forty years ago. "God made us to know Him, to love Him, and to serve Him in this world, and to be happy with Him forever in the next."

When I read that answer to that important question, it makes me reflect on how we need to get to know God now. This world is a sort of a preschool, or a kindergarten "readiness" class, if you will. The catechism's answer leads me to the conclusion that we should live this life getting ready for the next world, the next life.

As I remember my daughter's school days, my memory takes me back a step further to my own. The calendar on the wall said it was September 1956. My older brother and sister, Ben and Sue, had gone before me, and it was my turn. I had reached the ripe old age of five years, and it was my day to enter the first grade at St. John the Baptist Catholic School in Harvey, Illinois.

In those days there was no such thing as "school readiness." There were no such institutions as pre-schools, with very few of us even seeing the likes of a kindergarten class. Nope, it was just get your school bags and your lunch pail and let's get going. Those were the days when kids were tough.

Did I say tough? I can remember distinctly the first day that I had to go to school. It was traumatic. I was crying and screaming at the schoolyard for my mother not to leave me at this place. The nuns carried with them a mystique I didn't understand. All I knew was that I was being turned over to people who were dressed in black-and-white clothing and large headdresses and who didn't seem to have any hands or feet. What was my mother thinking, anyway? After all, I was only five years old, and now I had to spend seven hours a day away from my secure and safe home. *Wait, please! I'm not ready!*

Little did I know that those next eight years would instill in me a solid education in reading, writing, and arithmetic. But of even more significance, those years would shape my understanding of God and His kingdom.

The God I thought I knew would begin to be portrayed for me through these next eight years through instructional catechism, church experience, and my world.

Chapter Two

MY CROWN
OF JEWELS

I can remember having Sister Leona as our teacher for second grade. It was 1957–58, the year we were to make our first official confession and penance. We were taught that we had now reached the age of accountability. That of course meant that all of our prior sins were done out of ignorance. Now there was no excuse; we knew better.

We were told that we needed to account for all of our recent sins, those that were committed after we reached that infamous age of accountability. We needed to confess our sins to the priest inside a confessional box. There was a standard format to memorize in preparation for this. We needed to start our confession with the following words: "Bless me, Father, for I have sinned. I made my last confession . . ." At this point we inserted how long it had been since our last confession. Then we began listing for the priest all of our sins that we had willfully committed, both mortal and venial in nature.

One day, Sister Leona told us a story about how the kingdom of heaven operates. She said that each one of us begins life having an empty crown awaiting us. Every time we did something good, God put a shining jewel, such as a diamond or a ruby, into our crown. Conversely, every time we did something bad, God filled one of the spots in the crown with a black gem. Someday we would walk around heaven with our crowns. It would certainly be better to walk around with a crown full of shining jewels than black gems.

I got the picture. I imagined that God knew of every action, every transaction. He watched every one of our moves and recorded them. He kept score, and He would reward the good and punish the bad.

I could see where the sacrament of penance fit into the system. We needed to get those black stains off our souls. They needed to be erased before the great Bookkeeper in the sky closed His books. The system made a lot of sense. We were made clean by and through the ritual of infant baptism. That sacrament took away the guilt from original sin, the sin that we inherited from our first parents, Adam and Eve. It was now up to us to keep our slates clean. It was good to know that if the slate did become dirty, the system provided for a cleansing—kind of a second chance.

We were instructed that after we made our confession to the priest, it was his turn to give us our penance, our earthly punishment to help satisfy God for our transgressions. This was the time we held our breath. In all my years of going to confession and receiving penance I can only remember receiving one form of penance—I was instructed to say so many "Our Fathers" and so many "Hail Marys."

Interesting, when you think about it. I was instructed to recite prayers as my penance, my punishment.

I remember the day of my first confession to the priest in this dark, eerie confessional booth. I understood the teachings quite clearly. We were to tell all, hold nothing back. We were sinful human beings, and we needed to have our sins forgiven, or else we would suffer the just punishment of God. I was so nervous about making this confession that I wrote down all of my sins on a piece of paper. I wanted to make sure that when I went into the confessional to bare my soul, I did not forget one single sin. I was careful to be as quiet as possible when it came time to unroll the paper stuffed in my pocket. I did not want the priest to know that I came in with my sins written down on paper. After all, sins were supposed to burn an indelible mark on my brain, so they should just roll off my tongue.

But which actions were sins anyway? How can we tell that we have really sinned? We were well versed in the understanding of sins. We were told that sins were transgressions against God and the Church. God gave us His commandments to follow, along with the laws of the Catholic Church, and we were to follow these laws at all times. If we kept the laws we would be in good shape come judgment day. If we did not, we needed to get these sins remitted as soon as possible. For the Catechism told us:

> *Q#310: Is it enough to belong to God's Church in order to be saved?*
>
> A: It is not enough to belong to the Church in order to be saved, but we must also keep the Commandments of God and of the Church.

We were taught that there are degrees of sin, some serious, some not so serious. The less serious ones were called venial. The serious ones were titled mortal because this type of sin kills the sanctifying grace that we received at baptism. As it turns out it was the theologian Thomas Aquinas of the thirteenth century who really shaped our thinking and theology on sin. He classified sin as either *"fatal"* or *"non-fatal."* The catechism made the seriousness of mortal sin perfectly clear with this question and answer:

Q#55: Why is this sin called mortal?

A: This sin is called mortal because it deprives us of spiritual life, which is sanctifying grace, and brings everlasting death and damnation on the soul.

You cannot get much clearer than that. It was cast in stone. It was written in black and white for each of us to digest and believe. Mortal sin brings everlasting damnation on the soul! I thought about this a lot. I knew this to be an important teaching to understand.

We even had booklets that classified the degree of sin, mortal versus venial. This was extremely important, because an error in this matter could prove fatal for the poor sinner. After all, a mortal sin had the power to take away my crown for good. That is, if I died with an unconfessed mortal sin on my soul, I would stand condemned before God. I used to think, *I sure hope that booklet is right. After all, what if one of those venial sins listed on the left side of the page really belonged on the right side of the page with the mortal sins?* How did the Church know for sure God's measurement of the gravity of sins? I decided I just needed to trust in the Church for my salvation.

Haunting thoughts followed me deep into my adult

life. If I understood the teachings correctly, mortal or fatal sin seemed to be the critical area to avoid. If I could just stay out of this type of sin, I could keep my soul from the agony of an eternity in hell. For this was the sin that could cause permanent separation from God. But something just didn't seem right about this.

What about the guy who lived his whole life generating jewel after jewel for his crown and then the day before he died, he committed a mortal sin? Maybe he was sixty years old and he had fifty-nine-plus years of good living and then fell at the very end, unable to get to the confessional? Or worse yet, perhaps the poor soul did not know that the sin was indeed mortal. How does the system treat him? Would God send this man to an eternal punishment because of one major slipup at the end of his life?

Or what about the teenage girl who one day decided to skip Sunday Mass, then while playing hooky, she was run over and killed by a truck? It was the first Mass she willfully missed; it was the only mortal sin on her soul— would God condemn her to hell forever?

According to the system, the answer is yes to both scenarios! They were willfully committed and were left unconfessed as impenitent. It was clear from the teaching that the willful act of mortal sin destroys the sanctifying grace needed for entry into the kingdom of heaven. But what about their crowns of jewels? Certainly there were more diamonds than black gems. Is this the way it really is? Does this accurately describe the essence of God and His kingdom? Consider this: "Therefore no one will be declared righteous in his sight by observing the law; rather, through the law we become conscious of sin" (Romans 3:20).

The apostle Paul wrote this statement to the Jews living in Rome in the first century. Before he truly knew God, the apostle Paul was a high-level Jewish religious leader who hated anyone who proclaimed the name of Jesus as the Messiah of the Old Testament. He despised anyone who would proclaim himself to be "in Christ." Then one day, he was on his way to the city of Damascus to persecute the people claiming to be Christians.

He wanted to imprison a group of these people who were saying that this Jesus was the way to God. Paul thought this sect needed to be wiped out. He knew that an ordinary man could not provide the way for anyone. He believed that this man Jesus, who claimed to forgive sins, was a liar, a fraud.

You see, what Paul considered to be necessary for his salvation was strict obedience to God, to the Law, to the Scripture, to the temple, to the religious leaders, to good works.

Before he met the living Christ on the road to Damascus, Paul believed that people must *make themselves righteous* before this holy God! They needed to keep and follow the law. A faithful Jew needed to be circumcised as an infant. This ritual, as part of the process, made him part of God's family, he thought. People need to make themselves clean and then stay clean so that when God examines them on judgment day, they will appear righteous to Him.

It seems Paul preached this belief before he met Jesus, and then preached something very different after he met Jesus. Paul had labored so diligently to keep the Law. He now knew that by doing so he had actually been attempting to nullify the life, death, and resurrection of Jesus. For the first time, Paul was putting his complete trust in the person of Jesus Christ. Salvation was a free gift given to Paul by the grace of God—he didn't have to earn it. God had imparted a new life to His own enemy, Paul from Tarsus. Paul was overcome by God's love. He realized, for the first time, that he did not have to become righteous by keeping the Law. Christ Jesus did that for him by the Cross. Paul was now on a mission to make this miraculous truth known to others.

What happened? What would cause such a sudden change in a person's beliefs, beliefs that were steeped in religious traditions? Only days earlier, he had been looking to imprison anyone claiming Jesus' name. Now he was not only proclaiming His name, but telling others they must believe in Him in order to be saved. He was embracing the person of Jesus as the long-awaited Messiah of the Old Testament. Why? There was only one answer—Paul had met God. He experienced the deep and profound love of a God he had never truly known.

If there was ever a man who kept the Law, it was Paul! Listen to how he described himself.

> If anyone else thinks he has reasons to put confidence in the flesh, I have more: circumcised on the eighth day, of the people of Israel, of the tribe of Benjamin, a Hebrew of Hebrews; in regard to the law, a Pharisee; as for zeal, persecuting the church; as for legalistic righteousness, faultless. (Philippians 3:4–6)

A Pharisee lived in strict conformity to the Law. He studied the Law, he followed the Law, he lived the Law. As Paul said, he was faultless in keeping the Law. Not even a venial sin, or so he thought. Why did Paul now say that no one would be declared righteous by following the Law?

It says in the Bible that Paul started immediately to preach in the synagogues that this Jesus was the Christ—the Messiah proclaimed in the Old Testament. He seemed to surrender his old belief system that he was steeped in, the system that taught that a person had to make himself righteous before God, that strict following of the Law guaranteed entrance into the kingdom of heaven.

So if I believe in God, belong to the Catholic Church, am baptized, keep myself from serious sin, follow the commandments of God and the laws of the Church, and fill my crown with shining jewels—what more must I do?

We too must meet Jesus for the answer.

Chapter Three

PUNISHING THE WRONG MAN

In sixth grade the boys in our class began to get bold. That age of eleven and twelve is when boys start to exert their autonomy and stupidity at the same time. It was like any other day in class. Sister Bertha was conducting a lesson in geography. The lesson was quite boring to me. It would be much more fun if I could get the boys in the class to laugh a little, at least under their breaths. Sister Bertha was not accustomed to laughter in the classroom, especially during a lesson. So when Sister was at the board with the maps pulled down pointing out some far country, I decided to strike while she had her back turned.

Sister Bertha was by far the most stern nun in the whole school. We didn't mess with Sister Bertha if we knew what was good for us. We boys had a nickname for her, as we did for most of the nuns. We called her "Big Bad Bertha." That name hinted at power and might; it invoked fear at the sound. I think someone took our nickname and used it to create marketing hype for the famous golf club in the 1990s. Now the "Big Bertha" golf club is known for its power and might, able to hit golf balls mightily and swiftly, with precise accuracy. (We never got any credit or royalties for our ingenuity. We were just too far ahead of our time.)

We called Sister Bertha "big," but in sixth grade every teacher seems big. She was "bad." When she looked a boy square in the eye and squinted her steel-blue eyes, her look pierced his soul. She took no nonsense from her students, especially the boys. Her rugged leathery face was accentuated by her wire rim spectacles, which gave her a look somewhat like the character that Arte Johnson played on the TV show *Laugh-In*. Her thin lips always seemed to purse together, and she didn't smile very often. No one messed with Sister Bertha. No one.

In the early sixties, a favorite television show was called *Car 54, Where Are You?* The star of the show was Joe E. Ross, who played a floundering policeman named Tootie. He continually messed up his duties as a policeman, but he always came out smelling like a rose. Whenever he got excited about something, his eyes widened, his arms flailed, and he exclaimed, "OOO! OOO!"

That day in geography I thought it would be funny if I could make the sound that all the boys knew from this popular TV show during the middle of class. So at just the right time, when Sister Bertha turned away from the class toward the board, I let it rip—"OOO! OOO!" Sister whirled around and shouted, "Who said that?" She gazed over the class, carefully examining each boy's face. The girls were immediately exonerated from the process. Of course no girl would have ever ventured into such a dangerous and moronic stunt.

Sister was looking for the slightest expression of guilt among the would-be suspects' faces. She couldn't break us. We had carefully trained ourselves against this type of guerrilla warfare years before. After the muffled laughter died down, no one dared answer, especially me.

A few more moments went by, and when Sister turned to the map again to make a point, I once more called out "OOO! OOO!" She quickly turned, trying to catch the culprit before he could finish, but to no avail. Beaten again. Her face was fiery red with anger. At this point, any human being past the age of accountability and reason should have pushed himself away from the poker table and collected the winnings. But the boys in the class gave me that look—you know, the look that says, "Go ahead, I dare you to do it one more time." I bit. Every ounce of common sense and conscience was totally obliterated at that moment. Something in me said, "Just one more time!"

Once more I dared to be funny, or should I say obnoxious. I waited for some time to pass, maybe five minutes or so. I let it go once more, just at the right time when Sister turned her back. I came out with a super dare—"OOO! OOO!"

I will never forget what happened.

Sister immediately spun around, and she fixed her glare on poor Jamie Skorpinski, who was seated near her in the front row. Without warning, without question, she slapped him right across his face. Jamie said nothing, put his head down, and took my punishment. Sixth-grade boys have a secret code of honor that you never snitch on a friend, even if means takin' the rap. I felt ashamed of what I had done. Jamie did nothing wrong. I was to blame. I never did anything like that again.

Although Jamie took my punishment, and even though I felt ashamed, in a sense I was set free. I never received the punishment that I wholeheartedly deserved. Sister Bertha's wrath had been delivered, her anger appeased, though the punishment was delivered to the wrong guy. It should have been I who suffered the blow; it should have been I who was humiliated among all his classmates. How could I repay Jamie?

It wasn't my obedience that protected me from my teacher's wrath, but Jamie's punishment in my place. Our lack of obedience to God's law also keeps us from being called righteous. The apostle Paul said, "No one will be declared righteous in his [God's] sight by observing the law." Declared righteous—what does that mean?

A way to understand this is to break apart those two words, "declared" and "righteous."

Obviously, the word *declared* implies that someone will do the declaring. This we know to be done by God Himself. He is the one who ultimately declares, or judges, each of us to be just or unjust in His sight.

We can look to the Bible to try to understand this word *righteous*. It is helpful that the Bible gives us stories, by God, to help us understand how the kingdom of God operates.

I am sure you remember the story about Noah and the ark. But have you noticed that in this story the Bible says that Noah was *righteous*? It says, "Noah was a righteous man, blameless among the people of his time, and he walked with God" (Genesis 6:9). We get a hint that to be righteous also means to be blameless. To be without blame. To walk with God.

But wait, Noah wasn't always so blameless. We read later that he got drunk one day and lay naked in his tent in his drunken condition. But God said he was righteous before Him. How could God declare Noah righteous if he was not always righteous? How can God declare anyone righteous if Paul told us that *no one* would be declared righteous by trying to follow the Law? Now we need to start to comprehend something called *faith*. Hebrews 11 tells us that faith is what God counts as righteousness—faith in His righteousness rather than our own. About Noah, the text says, "By faith Noah, when warned about things not yet seen, in holy fear built an ark to save his family. By his faith he condemned the world and became heir of the righteousness that comes by faith" (v. 7).

Noah believed what God had told him. God told him that He was going to put an end to all the people who lived on earth. God told him to build an ark that would save him from the ravishing floods to come. Everything living on earth would perish. Noah believed God, but the others did not. Noah put his faith in the words of God; the others did not. His building the ark, the calling of animals, and his patience during the Flood demonstrated his faith in God. The others demonstrated their unbelief, because the Scriptures tell us their hearts were filled with evil motives all the time.

Noah put his faith in God. God saved him from the impending flood that destroyed the earth.

Noah was seen as righteous before God. But he was not made righteous by faithfully building the ark. He was not made righteous by getting his family to believe and help him. Instead, he was made righteous by God, through his faith, not by his works. He built the ark out of his faith in God's promises, not to attain his own righteousness. His building of the ark was a demonstration of his faith.

The Bible teaches us that we must be *made righteous*.

But the question then becomes—*How* can you and I be made righteous?

And furthermore, why do we need to be made righteous? Is there a flood to come? Is there an ark?

You and I cannot be made righteous by following the commandments, as Paul has warned us. Yet I encounter countless people who believe that we can attain the kingdom of heaven by keeping the commandments, doing good works. These people are doing exactly what Paul warned us against. They, through their actions, are trying to make themselves righteous before God! Mistakenly, they seek approval before God by their own actions. Often they are not even attempting to keep God-given laws, but those of their own making.

Could the worldwide destructive flood in Noah's day be anything like what Sister Malvina once talked about, a hell for the unbelieving? If this flood is a symbol of the hell to come, then what does the ark symbolize? What (or who) protects us from hell?

Let us examine one more story from the Bible regarding this idea of righteousness. It comes from the letter Paul wrote to the Romans in the first century. Paul was trying to explain to his fellow Jews who lived in Rome about the attainment of righteousness apart from their works of the Law. Paul reached into his Old Testament storybook and pulled out the story about Abraham.

Abraham was considered to be the patriarchal father of the Jews, the man God established His covenant with and to whom He gave His promises. The man of faith. So Paul, who knew the Jews were trying to *attain their own righteousness,* as he himself once did so earnestly, now gives them an argument centered on the *faith* of Abraham.

The Jews believed that a man had to be circumcised as a prerequisite of attaining righteousness before God. So Paul asked them if Abraham was declared righteous by God *before* he was circumcised or *after* he was circumcised? This is a trap question, posed like an attorney, in order to prove a point.

You see, if they said *after,* then they would be quickly reminded that this was contrary to what the Old Testament said. If they said *before,* then they could rule out circumcision as a prerequisite of being declared righteous by God. So the key is this: *When* was Abraham credited with righteousness? Paul said, "It was *not after,* but *before* [he was circumcised]!" (Romans 4:10, italics added). Thus Paul ruled out circumcision as a requirement for Abraham's righteousness. Circumcision, according to Paul, was merely "a seal of the righteousness that he had by faith while he was still uncircumcised" (v. 11).

What does this have to do with you or me? Plenty! We can begin to understand a few truths about us and God from these stories, such as:

(1) Unless we are made righteous, we will perish.
(2) We need to be made righteous by God.
(3) It is *not* the observing of the Law that makes us righteous.
(4) It is *not* rituals that make us righteous.
(5) Someone other than ourselves must be our righteousness for us.

Someone must be our *substitute.*

Jamie said nothing, put his head down and took my punishment. Jesus is my substitute. He sacrificed His very life for my errors. He took the rap for me, for He bore the wrath of God the Father, hanging on a cross for my sin.

"He was oppressed and afflicted, yet he did not open his mouth; he was led like a lamb to the slaughter, and as a sheep before her shearers is silent, so he did not open his mouth" (Isaiah 53:7).

Chapter Four

"ALWAYS BE IN;
NEVER GET OUT"

I can clearly remember a story that Sister Malvina told my first grade class one day. The Sisters were famous for inventing ways to make their point. Some of the nuns used their theological training to create order in the classroom. Often God was used as an all-powerful weapon to scare the living daylights out of us if we got to be unruly. But this story was not told because of a discipline problem. It was told because it was a basic doctrine of the Church.

Sister came up with an idea to try to communicate the reality of hell. Yes, that's right—the doctrine of hell starting in the first grade. Our theological training began early and swiftly. The Sisters didn't pussyfoot around by giving us only the heaven story for the first three grades, then when everyone was lulled into belief by the idea of heaven, pull the old bait-and-switch routine and bring in the really gruesome stuff of purgatory and hell. No, we jumped right in with the heavy stuff. We were tough back in those days. Once we sat through a lesson on hell we could handle just about any other doctrine that came our way.

Hell sounded like a terrible place: a place involved in the torture of people, a place with real fire. It was hard to get a picture of this place in my mind. It was difficult to fathom a place that has fire and is dark at the same time. After all, how much torment would a person be able to take? As a six-year-old, I tried to think of what this place could be like. I immediately thought of the dreaded dentist that I had to go to quite often as a child. The dentist himself was a nice chap, but what he had to do wasn't so nice.

When I was just five years old our family dentist said that I had more than twenty cavities that needed to be filled. For some reason, when I was very young I ran a high-grade fever. According to the dentist, this did something detrimental to the normal development of the calcium in my teeth. I was, I guess you could say, calcium-impaired. This, and my insatiable appetite for candy, apparently led to all those cavities at a young age.

The pain caused by the filling of the cavities, one by one, was excruciating. Medicine to deaden the pain was rarely used in those days. The feeling of those drills in my teeth went right through my spine. The dentist had to send my mother out of the room as I cried and screamed for mercy. The dentist had none; he merely covered my cries with his hand to muffle the sound until I stopped.

But somehow this place called hell seemed to be much worse, as hard as that was to conceive. I remember Sister giving us an effective illustration in her attempt to explain the difficult concept of eternity.

Eternity is a difficult concept for any person to understand, let alone six- and seven-year-old children. So after we heard about all the horrific events that go on in this dreaded place called hell, she told us something that I will never forget.

She told us that in hell, there looms a superlarge clock with a large pendulum that swings back and forth all the time. And when this pendulum swings it says in a loud deep voice, "Always be in" on the upside swing and "Never get out" on the downside swing. "Always be in; never get out." She kept repeating it. "Always be in; never get out." She told us this clock never stops repeating this to the people in hell, "Always be in; never get out. Always be in; never get out." I was frozen in my seat after I heard that story.

You may have had your own Sister Malvina experience. You may even be thinking that it was wrong to implant such terrifying ideas in impressionable little children. But I disagree; the story was effective. Not entirely accurate I am sure, but nevertheless effective. I was able to grasp the meaning of the words "always" and "never." I began to understand at an early age that our life is not a temporary one, but rather it is eternal. This story began to shape my thinking about my life. It always goes on; it never stops.

That concept calls for serious reflection. If it is true, then our life here on earth is like the dew on the morning grass in comparison. It is present for a short time in the morning, and then it is quickly gone. Seventy or eighty years on earth are nothing compared to an eternity to be spent in a place like hell. From that point in first grade, I was determined to understand how to keep myself out of this place called hell.

But as the apostle Paul once said, "When I was a child, I talked like a child, I thought like a child, I reasoned like a child. When I became a man, I put childish ways behind me" (1 Corinthians 13:11). As an adult, I must not think of hell as containing a clock with a constant reminder that a person is there for an eternity. However, I must think of a place called hell. I must surely reflect on the concept of an eternal life. Even if only half of what Sister Malvina taught about hell is true, then it is a place that calls for serious reflection on our part. I need an explanation that I can rely on to be true. I would not want to be deceived about eternal damnation to such a place.

But just when we need serious reflection and straight thinking, we tend to get mockery and deceit. Or worse yet, we don't talk about it. We ignore the reality. We are deluded into believing that only the worst, most corrupted beings who have walked this earth find their rightful place there. Only a few incorrigible degenerates end up there. Someone once likened it to the number of people in prison compared to the population as a whole. We hold on to these unbiblical thoughts, even though Jesus Himself taught that the road that leads to that place is wide and that many, not few, are on that road.

One deception prevalent today is the notion that this place does not exist. How ironic. Let's imagine there are hellish spiritual beings who have the ability and permission to roam the earth and who are trying to convince us that this place does not exist.

How would they do this in today's culture? Unfortunately, very easily. First of all, they would convince the learned that a place called hell is a leftover from medieval times and is not for intelligent thinkers in our modern world. The university professors have no place for a place called hell in their philosophy classes. Pity the poor soul at the university, either student or faculty member, who professes belief in an afterlife or a place called hell.

Second, the hellish spiritual beings need to deceive the cast that distributes our news via radio, television, and the print media (newspapers and magazines)—the very sophisticated, the very bright, the powerful and influential media personnel of our day. The thought of a place like hell is so foreign that it is held to be unenlightened, uneducated barbaric thinking.

The science community was convinced by the hellish spiritual beings generations ago. The idea of a scientifically unprovable realm is not even pondered for reflection. And when the culture looks to the scientific community for life's answers, the worlds of heaven and hell are unfortunately not even found in their vocabulary.

So we live in a culture that has been deceived about the place called hell. Further, our society elites mock anyone who professes its reality. The hellish spiritual beings have been strategic and systematic in deadening the conscience to this reality and to sin itself.

Something seems to blind our minds when we speak about the horrors of hell. Part of its truth is not considered by the thinkers of the university elite, the movers and shakers of the media, and the everyday person. Those who argue that a good, merciful God could not possibly send anyone to hell have left out a crucial truth. It involves the holiness and justness of God. It may be difficult for most university professors and the media to expound on the reality of God, since they rarely have a core belief to begin with. Furthermore, it quickly becomes even more uncertain to talk about a place called hell until a person first understands the holy nature of

God. The Bible declares Him to be "Holy, holy, holy." God is without sin. Sin is against the nature of God; it is against His very being. God is also just in the rendering of His judgments. No one can fool Him, no one can hide a false motive from Him, and no one can stand in the presence of God and declare himself to be holy.

So why did God create an awful, horrific place like hell, and why can we believe that it is real? Although I could expound for several pages on the answer to these questions, let it be sufficient to say that first of all Jesus Himself gives us most of our theology or understanding about a place called hell. He referred to it several times. If Jesus was fabricating the truth about such an important issue, then there really is nothing left to trust about what Jesus had to say about anything. We also must keep in mind that when the history of the world is culminated, and we are all whisked into eternity, God in all His glory and all His holiness will live without the hint of sin. God will remove, permanently, the unrighteous from the righteous. Thus those who have denounced God with their body, mind, and soul will be justly confined to a place that forever punishes their hatred for God. God does and will oversee the punishment of those in hell. Through their punishment, God will be found holy and just. And those who forever live with God in heavenly bliss will find God to be holy and just. God was, is, and always will be holy and just in all that He does.

For serious questions, I have found it best to turn to a serious teacher. In this instance, the teacher not only knows about hell, but He created it! Although Sister Malvina attempted to pass on some teachings on the place called hell, I believe that we need a good dose of adult teachings. There is no better place to look than to the Master Teacher—Jesus of Nazareth. If anyone can teach us the truth about an eternal, unseen, horrific place called hell, it is the One who truly knows of its existence and purpose! Let's examine what Jesus said about this place.

Jesus talked about hell frequently. He, like Sister Malvina, even told us a story about the place. The story is found in Luke 16:19–31. It is not, however, about a clock with a pendulum, but about a place of torment.

In the story we are told of two men. One was a rich man who dressed well and had wealth and influence. The other was a beggar who longed to eat a decent meal and yearned for someone to help him with his sickness. The rich man never paid attention to the beggar, even though the beggar lay at the entranceway to the rich man's house each day.

As the story goes, the beggar and the rich man both died. The beggar was so poor he could not afford a decent burial, so the angel came and took him to the place where Abraham is found, with God. However, the rich man, who could afford a burial, found himself in a place Jesus called hell. Jesus describes that place to us in the story by the rich man saying, "I am in agony in this fire." Is Jesus telling the truth with this story, or is He just trying to shock His listeners—or possibly both?

The rich man begs for mercy, but does not receive it. Abraham told him he received his good things while on earth. In contrast, the beggar, who trusted in God and begged for mercy in his earthly life, has now received it in this new place of comfort. Jesus also tells us some information about hell that the rich man didn't want to hear.

Abraham told the rich man that the place where he

37

was suffering was separated from the place where the beggar was being comforted. Furthermore, this separation is fixed. He will always be separated, never getting across! Always be separated, never getting across! Always be in, never get out.

Further, the rich man's request was denied. Abraham would not let the beggar leave paradise to warn the rich man's brothers on earth about hell. Jesus' answer to the rich man's request is insightful to you and me, even now: "If they [your brothers] do not listen to Moses and the Prophets, they will not be convinced even if someone rises from the dead."

Hey, wait, my catechism teachings are coming back. I know someone who left paradise; someone who came to earth to warn us about the agony of Hell; someone who rose from the dead!

His name was Jesus. Jesus was telling this story to not only describe the horror of hell, but also to make known to us that He and He alone can satisfy the holiness of God the Father. He alone can stand in our place of judgment? He must be our substitute!

Chapter Five

"YOUR WORD IS DOG"

Throughout grade school the Sisters had a teaching method that caused much fear and anxiety among the students. It was practiced with great frequency to determine if the students understood the lesson material under fire. Almost all of the students, especially me, dreaded hearing the words "Go to the blackboard!"

This was the time when the spotlight shined on an unfortunate few lined up at the blackboard at the front of the class. At this point a student's knowledge, or lack of it, was openly exposed to all of his classmates, and worst of all to Sister.

My very life and reputation hung in the balance. When the stress and tension of such an event neared, my mind froze. I tended to panic. What little knowledge I did have was locked deeply embedded in my frozen memory banks.

I can still remember squirming in my seat, with my hands sweating, trying to hide from the piercing eye of Sister Bertha. She had a knack of calling on those who seemed less prepared, less confident of knowing the material of the lesson.

One day, we reached that point in the day for our English lesson. Sister announced that several of the students would go to the board, and we would work on forming the plural of words. You know, the rules about when to use "s" and when to use "i-e-s" and all that good stuff.

For a fleeting moment, I hid my body strategically behind Monica. I felt somewhat safe as long as I did not move or make eye contact with Sister. She called out names of four students, and I knew that only three more would be called. There was only room for seven kids at the "totally embarrass yourself" blackboard.

I did not feel comfortable praying to God about this, since God seemed to be on the nun's side more than on that of us boys. I didn't want to chance it. After all, it was totally possible that God could cause Monica to sneeze or something and thus blow my cover. Besides, in the past Monica had seemed to provide a pretty effective shield.

Sister called Susan, then Frankie—and I thought, *One more and I am home free!* "And let's have Michael come up," she said. Rats! There was only one Michael in our class, and unfortunately that was me. I reluctantly made my way to the "board of ruin."

The assignment was simple. Sister would give each person a word to write down on the board. The student would then write the plural form of that word underneath it. Further, he would get the opportunity to explain the rule behind the plural form to the whole class. This last part was done just in case the student was faking that he knew the answer and happened to stumble upon the correct answer. Sister had all the angles covered.

I knew I had fallen short of the requirements, for I had not committed the rules to memory. I had neglected my previous homework assignment, and my hour of reckoning was near. I had been positive that going out to play baseball was much more important than committing some silly English rules to memory. I never saw girls playing outside after school. They were too busy working hard at making us boys look like idiots when we had to go to the board. Our victory was hitting a line drive over the telephone wires for a homer at the sandlot. The girls' victory was watching a boy squirm at the board in his ignorance.

I was banking for an easy word. She had given all the other kids their words. Finally she stood next to me. I held my breath. She said, "Your word is DOG."

My mind froze shut; I began to panic. The palms of my hands were sweating profusely. The white stick of chalk in my hand began to melt. My hands started to turn milky chalk white. The vault to my memory banks remained locked! Whenever fear and or anxiety flourished in my head, it automatically shut down any entryway to the brain.

What was the plural of DOG? It just couldn't be as simple as DOGS. Is this a word that gets the "i-e-s" on the end? It seemed to me that there first needed to be a "y" at the end of the word for that to happen. I was really beginning to lose it. Anxiety filled my very soul! My time to come up with an answer was running out. My heart was beating rapidly. My palms were wringing wet. My mind was totally blank. All the girls in the class pursed their lips together and smugly looked at me as if to say, "I wish I could help you, but Sister wouldn't like that." I was squirming big-time; the girls were approaching nirvana.

I could only think of one thing—get help and get it fast. As Sister was making her way down the board, stopping at each student and reviewing his work, I did the only thing I could possibly do to avert the imminent embarrassing disaster. I pleaded with Kevin Cassidy to feed me the correct answer. He had to do it secretly without the knowledge of Sister, who would soon be here.

Kevin wasn't exactly a Rhodes scholar; he was not the person to ask for this type of thing. His parents had recently immigrated to the United States, and Kevin struggled with the rules of the King's English. But I had no choice in the matter. Kevin was the only one who was close enough to hear my desperate cry for help, without being overly obvious.

Without hesitation, and with God surely knowing my dilemma, Kevin whispered to me the answer I needed. "It's doggies," he said. *Doggies?* I thought to myself. Can this be right? All of a sudden, the spirited tune, "How Much Is That Doggie in the Window?" raced through my mind. I found myself delighted, as I sang the tune over and over in my mind. God was surely confirming the answer given to me by Kevin. Yes! Of course, how obvious. It must be one of those words that gets the i-e-s on the end. That's got to be why Sister gave me this word.

I instantly wrote the presumed correct answer on the board and replaced the milky chalk on the long-running chalk ledge. Seeing that by now the chalk closely resembled a white pasty substance, the letters D~O~G~G~I~E~S looked like someone painted them boldly against the blackness of the board. But not a moment too soon. Sister had just finished with Frankie next to me. She told

Frankie to sit down, and then she moved right next to me. I'll never forget what happened next.

I was, by now, the only person remaining at the board, kind of like the finale at the fireworks show. It was the bottom of the ninth and I was up to bat with an 0 and 2 count. I can still remember the distinct smell of her perfume—something like a piercing pine tree.

She took one look at my answer on the board and tilted her head to the side. She looked at me for a moment, then she looked back at my word, then she glanced at the class. Assessing her mannerisms, I knew immediately that DOGGIES was wrong! I raised my hand to protect my face from the impending blow (you remember what happened to Jamie). But to my surprise she burst into laughter, and after she laughed, the entire class let out a roar. I couldn't believe it—I thought for sure that a severe punishment was in order. She kindly corrected my work, and we all had a good laugh. She truly had mercy on me.

Although I was the butt of the laughter, she had passed over my errors. I experienced her grace. That was just a shadow of God's grace. Consider what the apostle Paul tells us: "But God demonstrates his own love for us in this: While we were still sinners, Christ died for us" (Romans 5:8).

"Christ died for us"—I bet I heard that phrase hundreds of times while growing up. I understood what it meant historically. I understood that it was true because Sister and the Catechism said so, but I did not appropriate this truth in my heart. I did not really understand what grace meant.

This brings up many questions. What is the meaning of His death? Why did Jesus have to die at all? What

43

does something that happened two thousand years ago have to do with me?

I stated earlier that Paul made the argument that Abraham, although a sinner, was made right with God through his faith. We learned that Noah, although a sinner, was found to be righteous through his faith.

But what is this faith? We often define faith as simply a belief in *something,* maybe a body of teachings. But the saving faith the Bible talks about is a faith in *Someone.*

Let's review some biblical as well as historical facts about Jesus of Nazareth.

(1) Jesus was born without sin through the power of God Himself.
(2) Jesus lived His whole life without committing a sin.
(3) Jesus was human and Jesus was divine.
(4) Jesus was obedient even unto death on a cross.
(5) Jesus was accused and punished by death for things that He did not do.
(6) Jesus rose bodily from the grave three days after His physical death.
(7) Jesus lives today.
(8) Jesus was with God before the creation of the world.
(9) Jesus reigns from the right hand of God the Father in heaven.

Reread the above paragraph one more time, especially point #4. Jesus died for your sins. Think about this—He was *willing* to die for you. He did not do it out of obligation, but He did so out of His love for you and out of love for His Father. Jesus was willing to sacrifice His life to save yours and mine.

Jesus knew that without this perfect sacrifice, there is no salvation. There can be no other substitute. His life was uniquely perfect. It had to be perfect, because God demands perfection for our entry into the kingdom of heaven. We can enter through no other door! But a perfect sacrifice needs nothing more.

In fact there is no one, not one other who has the anointing, the power, and the perfect life to save us from the judgment of God against sin. You see Jesus was the only One to be without sin. He was the only One who could take our punishment on the cross. He and He alone is righteous before a holy God. You and I deserve to be on that cross. But He took our place. *He becomes our righteousness. And we acquire His righteousness through our faith in Him.* His perfect righteousness becomes ours, so that we can stand before His Father.

Sister Bertha withheld her punishment from me, a punishment I deserved. For some reason that I will never know, she had mercy on me. What shall we call this? We call it grace. God is gracious, but He cannot simply overlook our sins and continue to be righteous. That's why Jesus provided a way for God to exercise justice and grace. "Therefore, since we have been justified through faith, we have peace with God through our Lord Jesus Christ, through whom we have gained access by faith into this grace in which we now stand" (Romans 5:1–2).

But now, we need to come to understand what it means to experience God's grace. We need to grasp not only that Jesus died on the cross, for this is history understood by the mind. We need also to believe that He died on the cross for you and for me; for this is the essence of the Gospel that needs to be embraced by the heart.

Chapter Six

THE "PIT"

Our class had one boy who certainly was not Polish and who wasn't Caucasian. Anthony Guerrero transferred to our school around the fourth grade. He was the only Hispanic in the class and, as I recall, in the whole school.

Anthony was very soft-spoken, shy, and gentle as a lamb. He wasn't nearly as mischievous as we were. This fact, along with his being ethnically different from the rest of us, probably explains why Anthony was not a part of my close circle of friends.

I don't remember where he lived locally or where he moved from. I don't even remember ever seeing his parents. I never saw him again after graduation from eighth grade. But I do remember one event that involved Anthony.

As eighth graders, we were fortunate in having the only classroom that contained a stage, which was about twenty feet by fifteen feet. It was like going into a two-tiered classroom setting. About forty kids from the class sat in the normal seating area on the regular floor, and about fifteen sat on the elevated stage that the school used to put on plays or pageants for individual classes. (Yes, your math is correct; we did have fifty-five students in one class.)

The fun part of the stage was that it contained a trapdoor that led to a creepy place we nicknamed the "pit." It was like going down in a creepy, musty crawl space, with the dirt ground as your floor.

One day after lunch, and before the afternoon class was to start at 1:00 P.M., we got a great idea. About five of us boys were hanging around the stage area with nothing constructive to do. We thought it would be funny if we could find someone to throw down into the pit and then lock the trapdoor on him before Sister Tulia returned for class. Sister Tulia was also the mother superior, the principal.

We needed an easy target. Somebody neutral, not an enemy, not a close friend. So before poor Anthony Guerreo knew what hit him, four of us had grabbed him and hoisted him toward the pit. One of the boys moved the desk chairs that sat on the trapdoor. Frankie pulled the trapdoor open, and down went Guerrero, helplessly kicking and screaming.

What were we thinking? Did we think that he would politely sit down in that dark, musty place while the class continued? Did we think he would stay down there quietly until we graduated from eighth grade and then try to make an escape?

Stupidity was definitely a part of all this.

Suddenly someone shouted, "Sister Tulia is coming!" We quickly locked the pit door and rearranged the desk chairs in their proper places. We scurried to our regular seats as the rest of the class and Sister returned from their lunch.

We culprits were fighting back the laughter as we exchanged glances with one another. Sister was ready to start class. But there was big trouble in River City. Anthony began to cry out for help from the pit. He started to pound on his ceiling, which was the floor of the students who were seated on the stage. Everyone heard his faint, "Help me! Help me!"

Sister Tulia, not knowing exactly what was going on, followed the lingering cry toward the stage with a look of bewilderment on her face. She walked up on the stage, and she could hear that someone was stranded below. She told the students to move their desks, and she unlocked the trapdoor. I cannot describe in words the look of pity on her face when she saw poor Anthony staring up at her from the bottom of the "pit"!

She gave him her hand and pulled him out. Anthony was ever grateful for the rescue from that dominion of darkness. Anthony knew that if it were left to us, he would probably still be down there. I don't know why, but Sister Tulia never launched a full-scale investigation to hunt down the mastermind. Something tells me she didn't want to know. I think she gave the whole class a stinging lecture about how depraved one has to be to do this type of thing.

I was glad that she never pursued the criminals in this case. It would have been very difficult if we had had to go before Anthony's mother and father and explain why we threw their son into the pit.

Have you ever been rescued? I mean really rescued from something or someone dangerous. The people I know who have been rescued, those who have been saved from some impending harm that rendered them helpless, who had to rely on someone else to pull them from disaster, are very grateful to the person who saved them. They realize that without that person, they would have perished or would have been severely harmed.

Have you ever thought of your salvation as a *rescue?* In fact that is exactly what it is, a miraculous rescue. Someone must pull you from the flames, or from the pit. Someone throws you a rope just before you go under. You have to totally rely on that person's efforts, his mercy.

But now I have two questions for you. First, in regard to your own personal salvation, do you know what you need to be rescued from? And second, do you know who is your rescuer?

The answer to the first question may surprise you or even seem odd. You and I need to be rescued from ourselves!

That's right, ourselves. When we were born we inherited a condition that is naturally against the things of God. You might remember this teaching being called Original Sin. We have all inherited a naturally sinful disposition against God from our parents, who inherited this from their own parents, and so on and so on.

I have some good news for you and some bad news. The bad news first.

This natural disposition toward sin will continue throughout our entire life until someone rescues us from this "pit." We become a slave to its calling. We are helpless and literally powerless to release our own selves from this prison. We are left to do only one thing, like Anthony—cry for help.

We are dependent upon the rescue attempt. We are dependent upon the mercy of the rescuer. We have nothing within us that can aid us in the rescue attempt. We are sinking deeper and deeper into the pit, hoping that someone will save us.

Now here's the good news. We do have a rescuer. We are not left stranded. Our rescuer is a perfect One. He not only rescues us, but He is the One who can make us new people. His rescue includes giving us a new nature and a resultant new life. He can take away the effects and the consequences of the old. He sets us free from our helplessness. He, like Sister Tulia, unlocks the door of the pit, reaches down, and pulls us out. He is delighted to give us a new life. He is delighted to give us *His life!*

Who is this rescuer? He has a precious name. His name is JESUS!

Reflect a moment on what the apostle Paul told the Romans:

"You have been set free from sin and have become slaves to righteousness. . . . For the wages of sin is death, but the gift of God is eternal life in Christ Jesus our Lord" (Romans 6:18, 23).

And now here's the really good news. This new life is a *gift* from God. It is not something that you must earn! It is nothing that you must pay for. For if you must earn it or pay for it, the gift can no longer be a gift.

How does a person attain this life? By accepting God's grace.

Chapter Seven

MARIE
THE HUN

The Sisters had many unique methods for keeping order in the classroom. That seemed to be an important goal for each of them: keeping order at all places and at all times. The Sisters employed many offensive weapons to make sure that chaos never crept into their classrooms.

One of the methods employed by the Sisters was to have an army of what I call "professional snitches." The boys had a unwritten pact never to squeal on a fellow mate. The penalty would have been suffering backlash and ridicule for being a "squealer." Nothing was worse than being pegged as a rat by your male counterparts.

This had a power of its own. For if you never turned in a brother, then the officiating would be severely limited and based only on what one adult was able to see. However, the nuns always seemed to be a step ahead of our thinking and maneuvers. They had a large volunteer army to help expose our delinquent deeds. Most of the girls seemed to delight, yes, delight, in letting the Sisters know which boy broke the law!

Although the girls never flaunted it, they seemed to take great pleasure in blowing the whistle on some wise guy in the class. I never saw them brag to one another saying, "Hey, did you see me nail Tommy?" or "It was so great to see Sam get what he had coming." But there was a certain smug attitude, like "Don't mess with me or I'm going right to Sister!" That was a viable weapon.

One day in fifth grade, Sister had to leave the room for some reason and run back to the convent. It was never explained to us why they went back there during the school day. It remained one of those nun mysteries, like, Did they really have a head of hair underneath their habits?

Before she departed Sister warned, "No one is to talk while I am gone." In other words, Thou shall keep thy mouth shut! Although to us Sister seemed to be omnipresent, she nevertheless asked Marie Jakubowski to stand up by the board while she was gone. Marie was then instructed to write *anybody's* (code language for drop the "d"—any boy's) name down who talked or was disruptive while she was gone. Sister gave us some menial assignment to do while she was gone, and off she went.

Marie flew to the board and grabbed the chalk. She seemed eager to nab her first male victim. She panned the class with sharp attentiveness. Marie was no patsy. She could likely pin just about any boy to the wrestling mat if the challenge was ever made. The boys respected her and, quite frankly, feared her. She was now given official power and authority.

I don't know what possessed me to do what I did. It was unlikely that I would have said anything ordinarily. But when Sister made a clear command to keep silent during that timeframe, something inside me seemed to entice me to do just the opposite.

At just the right moment, when I thought Marie wouldn't see me, I stood up and said something stupid as fast as I could, like in two seconds, and then sat down. I did it. I broke the law. Best of all, she didn't even see me. She was looking the other way, and I pulled it off.

But my brilliant plan was about to come unraveled. Although Marie "the Hun" didn't see me and didn't know who had spoken, her girlfriend Theresa "the Snitch" did. And so did Gloria "the Tattler" who sat next to me. And before I knew what hit me, the mod squad ratted on me. Marie promptly wrote my name up on the board for everyone to see. I was mortally wounded.

At the very moment Marie finished writing my name on the blackboard, Sister darted back into the room. I had no time to bargain, no time to negotiate. The first thing Sister did was thank Marie for her excellent police work. All the girls seemed to rejoice in another victory, for there were no girls' names written upon the death list. Once again they were found innocent of any wrong-doing, whereas, once again, the boys' record was tarnished with a willful violation of the law. Who would defend me? No one; justice was served. I was condemned by the law.

The Ten Commandments were given to us by God, through Moses. These laws were passed down and recorded for us in the Old Testament. These commandments were broad in nature. After all, only ten were given. The first four had to do with our relationship to God. The last six were given in reference to our relationship with other people.

If I understood my teachings correctly, in order to

gain entry into God's kingdom I needed to keep my name off the eternal blackboard in heaven. Keep the slate clean. Then surely God would look at the clean blackboard *and* my crown of jewels. If God liked what He saw, I was in. If my name kept coming up on the blackboard and my crown was full of black gems, then I could be in big trouble. I needed to gain eternal life by following the Law, by keeping the commandments, by obeying the laws of the Church.

But why did God give us His commandments? What purpose do they serve?

Do you want to hear something surprising that the apostle Paul tells us about the commandments and our salvation? Consider this: "I found that the very commandment that was intended to bring life actually brought death. For sin, seizing the opportunity afforded by the commandment, deceived me, and through the commandment put me to death" (Romans 7:10–11).

Let's stop here for a moment to catch our breath. *You mean to say that the very commandments that I am trying to follow to gain eternal life with God are the same commandments that actually condemn me?* Yes, that is exactly the point God is making through the apostle Paul!

Do not misunderstand Paul on this point. He is not saying the commandments are bad. In fact, they are holy; they are in themselves a reflection of who God is. The commandments reflect His being; they make known His very nature. His laws are holy and good.

However, we are not holy and good. Here is a point worth considering: If you think that you can merit eternal life with God because you are doing your best to follow the commandments, then you have been deceived by your own sin. It is impossible to stand before a holy God and to proclaim that you did an outstanding job of keeping the laws. This, in itself, would obligate God to reward you with the kingdom of heaven.

I have news for you. If we can obligate God, then there is no such thing as grace! Remember what the apostle Paul called our salvation? He called it a gift—a gift from God so that no one can boast about his entry into the kingdom of heaven. It is God who gives life. We cannot earn this new life—it is His gift, out of His grace, to us!

If salvation is a gift, then it cannot be earned. If salvation can be earned, then it is not a gift. Both propositions cannot stand as truth at the same time.

So you see, if we stand before God without a defender, the Law we have broken will be there to condemn us, not to save us. If we are boasting and trusting in our obedience to the Law to save us, then something has deceived us. It is our sin that deceives us, for it is impossible to keep the Law perfectly. Deceit makes something that is truly condemning us appear to be saving us. Deceit makes something that is false appear to be true.

Consider again the idea of trying to attain your own righteousness by doing your best to obey the Ten Commandments and the laws of the Church. What does God tell us about this idea? Read this truth written by the apostle Paul: "I do not set aside the grace of God, for if righteousness could be gained through the law, Christ died for nothing!" (Galatians 2:21).

Yes, you read that verse correctly. If we can become righteous on our own, by following the laws of God and the Church, then we are in fact nullifying the death of Jesus on the cross! If we are trying to gain entrance into the kingdom of heaven by being good people, we will fail. This testifies that our faith is in ourselves or in a religion. But it is impossible to keep the Law perfectly. Our sinful nature has enslaved us under the Law. We are, in fact, prisoners of the Law. We need to be set free. We need a rescuer, a perfect rescuer.

There is only one person in all of history who has attained perfect righteousness through the law—the person of Jesus Christ. We somehow need His righteousness to be applied to us before we stand before this holy, holy, holy God. We need our life to be transformed by His. We somehow need to appropriate His life to ourselves. We need to lose our life for His. We need to start over, to start again.

Chapter Eight

I TELL YOU
THE TRUTH

A special place at St. John's parish called the grotto gave special tribute to Mary. It was somewhat of a stone shrine along with a garden of well-groomed bushes, trees, and flowers. The grotto was built right between the church and the school, a mere twenty feet or so from each of the buildings.

One day, not long before our eighth-grade graduation date, was bright and very springlike. The birds were chirping, and the trees and flowers were starting to bloom. It was a time for spring-cleaning and working out in the yard to get ready for the full bloom of beauty.

I remember the morning well. We knew we would be graduating from school within the next few months. That notion seemed to give us a feeling of liberation and boldness. One day, probably during a free time or recess, we were congregating on the stage area of the eighth-grade classroom near the windows. We all noticed an old-looking man bent over and working in the garden of the grotto. We knew all the people who hung around the church and school and certainly knew everyone who worked there. But we did not recognize this man. The man was wearing a straw hat and old tattered clothes, and he appeared to be busily weeding the garden. Our curiosity got to us, because we could not see his face.

Wanting to draw laughter from the boys who were gathered around the window, Frankie called out, "Ragman, hey, ragman." We all kind of nervously chuckled as we awaited the response of this poor man. The man didn't respond to him; he apparently didn't hear him. So Frankie decided to increase his decibels. He shouted, "Ragman, hey, ragman." The man heard him that time.

The man slowly got up from his knees and turned toward the windows, and we couldn't believe what we saw. It wasn't some old man who was hired to pick the weeds from the garden for a day; it was the *monsignor,* the head priest, Father Grembowicz! Yikes! We were dead!

We almost fainted; our hearts were in our throats. Sister was sure to find out about this. How could we know? He didn't look like who he was. Why would the senior priest be digging in the garden wearing old clothes and an old hat? That's not the way we knew him.

In my Catholic upbringing, I thought I knew about the first person called God the Father. I thought I knew more about the second person of the Trinity called God the Son. But I knew the least about the third person called God the Holy Ghost. The word *ghost* implied something spooky to me.

But what is the role of the Holy Ghost, now usually called the Holy Spirit? Does He just sort of float around? Does He zap people? Who is He? The one person who gave us the most detailed teachings on the Holy Spirit was Jesus Himself.

Jesus talked about the Holy Spirit in John 3:1–21. The story is about a man who came to Jesus at night. This particular man marveled at what Jesus was doing. But what this man really wanted to know was, What did Jesus have to do, if anything, with God's plan of salvation? Before the devoutly religious man, named Nicodemus, could even formulate the question, Jesus gave him the answer to his heart. Jesus said to Nicodemus, "I tell you the truth, no one can see the kingdom of God unless he is born again" (v. 3).

You might think Jesus should have said something like, "I tell you the truth, no one can see the kingdom of God unless he (a) has been baptized, (b) keeps My commandments, (c) keeps the holy days and feasts, and (d) stays out of serious sin." But that is not what He said in reference to seeing the kingdom of God.

In other words, if you want to know God as Father, you need to be made able to see who Jesus really is. If you are looking for the kingdom of God, but you do not acknowledge that Jesus is who He claimed to be, you will not see or understand the kingdom of God.

Nicodemus, being highly religious, knew about God and the promise of a coming Messiah. He just didn't know how Jesus fit into the picture. To Nicodemus, this Jesus seemed to have power from God Himself. His teachings were amazing, and His miracles were like no other. Who was this man really? This is what Nicodemus was asking.

In order to understand the answer from Jesus, we should first look at who Nicodemus was. He was a high-level Jewish religious leader, belonging to the Pharisaic order. Pharisees took it upon themselves to separate themselves from others by strictly (and I mean strictly) following all of the laws and commandments. By the way, they had hundreds more laws of Judaism to follow in addition to the Ten Commandments of Moses, and they added some of their own laws as well.

So Jesus began telling this religious leader/teacher about entering the kingdom of heaven. He first told Nicodemus, a grown man, that he must be born again. Nicodemus, who found the statement rather confusing, correctly replied that it was impossible to reenter his mother's womb to be born a second time. Jesus got a little more specific when He replied, "I tell you the truth, no one can enter the kingdom of God unless he is born of water and the Spirit. Flesh gives birth to flesh, but the Spirit gives birth to spirit" (John 3:5–6).

Jesus once said, "What is impossible with men is possible with God" (Luke 18:27). And this is one of those situations when we can directly apply this truth. It is impossible to see the kingdom of God if man is left to himself.

The fact is, we need the intervention of God in order to be able to see and enter the kingdom of God. Again, we need to be saved from ourselves. Enter the Holy Spirit, who is God Himself! Now we begin to see the *role and work* of the Holy Spirit.

Jesus told Nicodemus that he had to be born not only of water, the natural cleansing water that accompanies our physical birth into this world, but also of the Spirit. He made it clear that just as water accompanies our birth into the natural world, the Holy Spirit accompanies our birth into the spiritual world. Physical people can only give birth to physical people. This is the natural reproductive cycle provided to us by God.

But it is God, and God alone, who makes it possible

to open our eyes to the kingdom of God. It is God and God alone who gives us supernatural birth into the kingdom of God. But, you may ask, how does He do this? This is not easily explainable. Keep in mind, we are faced with the limitations of a finite, natural being trying to explain the work of an infinite, supernatural Being.

By an act of pure mercy from the Father, the Holy Spirit reveals to us the Son. This is the Trinity operating as one. When we see the Son, what do we see? We see a holy, holy, holy God in human flesh. We see the Son who bore nail marks in His hands and feet.

Through the convicting work of the Spirit, we realize, for the first time, that we are the cause of those nail marks. We see, through this new birth, things that we have never seen before because once we were dead to the things of God. We had a dead spirit because of that which separates us, our sinful unbelief.

But now we need to be made alive, alive to Christ! This is what Jesus was explaining to Nicodemus. He was telling him that to see the kingdom, one's eyes and heart must be opened. A dead spirit must be made alive. We are to trust in God for our eyes to be made open and for our hearts to be softened. For it is God, alone, who is able to take a hardened religious heart and make it into a truly soft spiritual one. It is the role of the Holy Spirit to *remove the scales from our eyes*. This is why the songwriter of "Amazing Grace" wrote this verse, "Amazing grace! How sweet the sound, That saved a wretch like me! I once was lost, but now am found, was blind, but now I see."

Second, it is the Holy Spirit who convicts us of our sins. It is for this reason that we may weep for our sins. We meet a God who is without sin, a perfect God. We experience His love for us and see that here is a love that runs deep. For the first time, we realize that while we were enemies of Him, He died on a cross for us. We are overwhelmed with His *love* and His *forgiveness*.

We experience new life. A cleansing. A life that we have never known before. We have found something so precious that we are willing to give up our old life in order to preserve this precious new life given to us as a gift. We are willing to turn from our old life, an old life that is offensive to a holy, holy, holy God.

This new birth is not natural. No, it is supernatural. It is a birth from God Himself, through the power of the Holy Spirit. It is the Spirit who gives this life. This is what Jesus wanted Nicodemus to know and understand. This is what God is calling you to understand about Himself and yourself.

It is God who gives life by His grace. We are the recipients of this new life. We appropriate this life through our faith alone in His Son, and in His Son alone. We turn from an old life that is unable to see the kingdom of God. We turn and live a new life, a life that springs from our salvation. A life following in the path of the Son. A life that embraces the kingdom of God. A new life caused by God Himself, through His power.

Consider the outcome of what the apostle Paul told the Romans: "Therefore, there is now no condemnation for those who are in Christ Jesus, because through Christ Jesus the law of the Spirit of life set me free from the law of sin and death" (Romans 8:1–2).

This is profound. It is saying several things: Paul was saying that those "in Christ" no longer stand condemned. They are saved from the wrath of God's judgment against sin. They are saved from God's judgment of eternal punishment. Why? Because, by the grace of God, they have the pure righteousness of Jesus Christ imputed to themselves. If I am in Christ, God no longer sees my dirty rags of righteousness. He now sees His Son whom He loves. He is now re-creating me to be conformed to the likeness of His Son. God is turning my heart toward Himself.

However, those who are not free from the coming condemnation are those who are trying to earn their way into heaven by following the Law. These same people are nullifying the work of Christ Jesus on the cross. They are trying to *attain their own righteousness*. Instead, *Jesus* becomes our righteousness, our holiness, and our Redeemer.

But those "in Christ" are no longer under the condemnation of the Law. Why? Because they are now found in the One who is righteous, the *only* One who satisfied the Law perfectly; the one and only Jesus Christ. Jesus has been made known to them. How? By the power and testimony of the Holy Spirit.

Listen, my beloved friend: When God looks at you on judgment day, you do not want to be standing alone. But if you have placed your trust in Christ, the Father will instead see you "in His Son Jesus Christ." Jesus will have saved you from yourself. His death on the cross will cover over your sins by satisfying the punishment for them. God will only see the righteousness of His Son, rather than your transgressions, which have been forgiven. Jesus can and will be *your* defender, your Redeemer!

I am trusting God that the teachings of Jesus will be meaningful to you as you reflect on what He says to you and to me, "I tell you the truth, no one can see the kingdom of God unless he is born again."

We need to apply this teaching to our own life. The Holy Spirit's role is to reveal Jesus, the true Jesus of the Bible. Unfortunately, I think some of us see Jesus as "the ragman." We see Him, but we don't see Him for who He truly is. He can only be worshiped and adored when we truly know Him as our defender, our Savior, our life, and our God. We must be given new eyes by the Holy Spirit before we can see Him!

Chapter Nine

A TRANSFORMATION

In the third grade, two brothers transferred into our class. Their last name was Stuart. I don't remember their first names, because we always called the Stuart boys by their last name. Their family moved up to the Chicago suburbs from somewhere in the southern states.

It was difficult for any new kid to transfer into our environment and fit in. The students at our school were predominately of second-generation Eastern European heritage, and practically all the kids grew up in the same neighborhood and came from blue-collar families. We often did not make the transition very easy for newcomers. It was especially difficult to transfer if the newcomer was different from us.

Not only did the Stuart boys not have a Polish heritage like most of the rest of us did, but they also had something that made them stand out even more. They had a personal hygiene problem. It was obvious that their household did not practice the art of regular bathing or grooming.

I can still remember, in my smelling memory banks,

the putrid odor that permeated the classroom each day. Their odor made their presence known wherever they went. Some days were worse than others. Some days it was difficult to come within five feet of their presence without having to hold my nose. I exaggerate not!

They also seemed to live in a home without combs. Their matted hair seemed to be "parted" on whatever side they had slept the previous night. Their clothes were wrinkled and stained. You can imagine the snide remarks and the ridicule that we heaped upon the Stuart boys. Since we often came up with nicknames for people in the class, we unashamedly nicknamed them the "Stinky Stuarts." How juvenile! It was a nasty nickname for a nasty smell.

The Sisters were tolerant up to a point. One day Sister Maxie could take it no longer. I think she had done her best not to call much attention to the Stuarts before this. However, Sister was at her wit's end. In the middle of class one day, she asked the boys flat out, "Why don't you boys take better care of yourselves?" I don't remember their response. They probably were embarrassed. Maybe they thought they looked fine to the world. I don't know for sure. All I know is that Sister came up with an on-the-spot solution to the problem.

Before I knew what hit me, Sister told *me* to take the Stuart boys to the back cloakroom and do something about their appearance. Now! What could I possibly do? Surely she was kidding. It must be an idle threat in order to motivate them to clean up their act. Nope, she was serious.

I got up from my seat, not having a clue as to what I could do. Why did she pick on me? Sister did seem to like my hair, which resembled a hybrid of the hairstyles of Elvis Presley and Paul Anka. But I really didn't want to be in a small enclosed cloakroom with the Stinky Stuarts. All the kids watched intently as I made my way back to the cloakroom, with the Stuart boys trailing close behind.

Although I didn't want this job, surprisingly the Stuart boys did not seem to resist the notion. They even seemed to trust that I could help them in some way. More likely they knew that they must either comply to some degree or face the wrath of one very unhappy nun. I looked around the cloakroom in desperation as to what resources might be available for this seemingly impossible request.

The only thing in the room, besides a whole rack of coats and boots, was a bucket of water. This was not ordinary water. This was the water used to clean the blackboards each day after class. The water in the bucket had been used several times that week, and it had developed a chalky composition. However, since I needed something to create with, it was my only ticket.

I could not do anything about their putrid odor at this time. I could not do anything about their wrinkled, stained clothes at this time. But I could do something about their hair! So I whipped out my own trusty steel comb, dipped it in the bucket, and went to work.

After about fifteen minutes the Stuart boys and I emerged from the cloakroom. Everyone in the class turned around and gasped in amazement. A couple of the girls let out squeals. Sister Maxie beamed with a smile, and I could hear a muffled, courteous laugh. No one could believe it. It was the first time anyone had seen the Stuarts with their hair fashionably combed. It was a transformation.

Their hair was slicked back, with the chalky water acting like a super hair spray. Not a hair was out of place. They had a crisp part on the left side of their heads. They had a wave in the front, with the sides combed back. Because their hair was still wet, it had a shine to it. Paul Anka and Elvis Presley would have been proud. Of course the chalk had a stiffening effect on the hair, making it almost brittle to the touch—there was no way their hair was going to move out of place for the rest of the day. But my work was done. Sister was pleased. The Stuart boys were seen as new, acceptable. They had been shown a new way.

This simple story exemplifies how God operates. He is in the business of making things anew, making us acceptable. God is getting us cleaned up. But He doesn't just clean us up a little; He makes us brand new. He likes order; He delights in the obedience of His children; He likes being a Father to us. But if we are going to talk about God in these terms—Father and children—then we have to understand something about God.

God is a person. He is personal. We are created in His image and likeness. We are created as persons. Thus when we think of God and we think of ourselves as children, we have to think in terms of a personal relationship: a relationship a Father would want with His children, a relationship a child would want with his Father.

Have you ever thought about this? Have you ever thought of having a personal relationship with God Himself?

Each day a man came home from work and greeted his wife and his son. His wife instructed the boy to always greet his father, because this is what children should do. Each day the son greeted his father with these words, "Hello, Father, I am glad that you are home." His mother instructed the boy to ask his father for food each day at the dinner table, because this is what he was supposed to do. Each evening at the dinner table the boy would say, "Dear Father, would you fill up my plate?" The mother also advised the child to say good night to his father, since this was a rule to be followed in the household. So each night before he went to bed the boy said, "Good night, Father, I'll see you in the morning."

The boy was misled into thinking that these things would please his father. This went on day after day. Night after night. Every day the same words. The same inflections in the voice, the same routine, day after day. The boy knew many things about his father, but the boy never knew his father. There was no personal relationship!

The truth is, many of us know *about* God, but we don't have a personal relationship *with Him*. We are often misled to believe that we cannot have or do not need a true relationship with God.

In our story, what type of relationship did the son have with the father? Little to none. It was rote, built on a sense of duty and obligation. The father did not seek a relationship with the son, and the son didn't know how to build a relationship with the father.

But in our case, God the Father sought relationship with us and made a personal relationship for us possible through His Son, Jesus Christ. We need to be first convicted in our hearts that we do not have a true relationship with God, that we are estranged. Many of us sort of know this, but we can't verbalize it. We can't explain the emptiness in our lives, though we know it's there. That emptiness is sometimes all-consuming.

Remember the Catechism:

Q#6: Why did God make you?
A: God made me to know Him.

In fact, although we may not express it verbally, we try to fill that void in our lives with people, positions, and things. We take different paths, different roads. We are just trying to find the road that leads to happiness, to fulfillment, to joy. You may be on one of these roads right now. You are looking for something to fill that emptiness in your life, something to fill that ever-present void. Something is missing, but you can't seem to find it. You are crying out deep within your heart, "Somebody help me!"

How do we experience what God wants for us? Listen to what Jesus told a group of men.

> People were bringing little children to Jesus to have him touch them, but the disciples rebuked them. When Jesus saw this, he was indignant. He said to them, "Let the little children come to me, and do not hinder them, for the kingdom of God belongs to such as these. I tell you the truth, anyone who will not receive the kingdom of God like a little child will never enter it." (Mark 10:13–15)

How should we understand this? Are we to try to be like children all over again? Should we be childish in our thinking, in our actions, in our stature? Is this what it takes to enter the kingdom of heaven? No, obviously, this is not what Jesus is teaching.

Jesus was indignant about the ignorance being displayed by the disciples. They were prohibiting the trust of the people who believed that this Jesus had the power to dispense the blessings of God Himself. The disciples were inadvertently trying to prohibit the glory of God from being known. Jesus was indignant because the disciples were treating Jesus as if He were not directly approachable. They believed He was not accessible to the average person—and especially not to the lowly people, the less important, such as children.

These same lowly and less-important people were exhibiting their faith in the person of Jesus. Jesus welcomed this. He even stopped to rebuke His own followers, because apparently they did not understand that the kingdom of God was not appropriated by power or status, nor by riches or intelligence. Instead it is appropriated by faith, childlike trust in the person of Jesus Christ.

Jesus was telling His followers that entry into His Father's kingdom is gained *by faith,* not by one's own power or by one's deeds. It is not inherited by earthly riches or earthly stature in the community. In fact, Jesus warned the disciples that unless they demonstrated such innocence and trusting faith, they too could not see the kingdom. Jesus called for them to have childlike faith.

Can you remember how a little child trusts? Children inherently trust their parents. They trust for their food, clothes, and shelter. They trust that if they are hurt their parents will tend to them. They trust their parents to give them love. They explicitly trust in these two people, their father and mother. It is the nature of the child to trust, to be dependent on the wisdom and resources of the parents. Children are not relying on a system; they are trusting in their parents. Obviously, if little children were left to themselves they would perish.

This is what Jesus is teaching us by this story. We

need to approach God with trust, dependence. A trust that comes from the heart, not just from the head. A faith that permeates our very soul. A faith, not in a system that saves, but in a person who saves—a man who sacrificed His very life to save us. A person who has the power to transform our very life and soul. We go into the closet stained, smelly, and with our hair in chaos. We emerge from the cloakroom with a new life. We don't emerge with just a new look. We are literally transformed; we are made anew in our inner being. We are a new creation.

This transformed life is a demonstration of the power of God. It is made possible only by God's grace. We gain access to this new life through our personal faith in Jesus. We can have peace with God, by His grace, through our faith in the person of Jesus Christ!

Many of us are searching for this peace in our lives. We long for real, unconditional love. We carry a weight on our shoulders that we cannot bear. We need someone to lift this yoke from our shoulders. Only Jesus can lift this guilt. It is only Jesus who calls us to Himself—and we are to approach Him with a childlike trust that He can save us.

Is God calling you to this type of childlike faith in Jesus? God desires a personal, not a merely ritualistic, relationship with you, through the Son!

Chapter Ten

PHYSICAL
FITNESS

All I can tell you is that it was unbelievable. It topped by far our most daring risk. It was an absolute violation of every conceivable convention. In one fell swoop, we broke every protocol of order ever established by St. John's school. It was absolute chaos.

It was seventh grade. It was springtime, and it was an afternoon recess like none other.

Our parochial school, like many others in the 1950s and 1960s, did not have a physical education program to speak of. The school's idea of physical fitness was a recess break and a lunch break. During these times we were allowed to play on the playground property that was directly across the street to the east of the school, church, and convent. Although the school itself faced the west, the sisters' home, the convent, faced the east—the playground area.

That is an important logistic to keep in mind as you read this story.

During recess and lunch break, we played the normal games played by kids who grew up in the fifties and early sixties. The girls did a lot of jump rope, hopscotch, and swinging on the swings. I was always amazed at how they were able to keep their balance as they started to swing two ropes simultaneously. It always seemed that one of those ropes would surely catch a girl's foot, if not her neck! Girls in those days didn't run track or play basketball, baseball, or volleyball. Whatever the girls did at recess, they always seemed to stay out of trouble.

On the other hand, we boys were determined to exhibit our athleticism through various games, such as Pom-Pom-Pullaway (which you may remember as Red Rover). Someone divided up the sides equally between the number of players. Each team then took its position on the field about forty-five feet apart. Each team stood facing the other, while holding hands with one another. Thus each team made a human chain that the other team tried to break open with the opponent sending a runner crashing into the line with all his might and strength. If the runner broke the chain, he returned to his team's side, but not before he grabbed the other team's strongest player to take back as a new teammate. If the runner was caught by the human chain and failed to break through, then he was absorbed into their chain to make it longer. Whichever team had the longest chain at the end of the game was the winner.

Sometimes we played Buc-Buc (a game not developed for the faint of heart) or some other game. This was the extent of our physical education in the eight years of grade school. There was no gymnasium. And other than having basic playground equipment, we had no formal training in anything physical. So we improvised with our own games.

One day, for some unknown reason, we had our first

taste of a formal physical education program—which was also our last. Although no one ever dared to ask why, the Sisters, maybe out of guilt, or maybe out of experimentation, one afternoon decided to conduct a physical education class.

It was a pleasant, sunny spring day. We had a special assembly of the fifth, sixth, and seventh grades out on the playground. Someone had heard that the Sisters were going to try out a new idea in physical fitness. Our curiosity was piqued. So as we made our way out to the playground across the street from the convent, we all gathered grade by grade, boys on one side, girls on the other.

The Sisters had set up a record player and large speakers, something like you might have seen at a Barnum & Bailey's ringside circus. This was totally unprecedented. The Sisters instructed us to form two lines, running north and south, and to pay attention to the instructions from the record blaring through the loudspeakers. This was unreal!

The record player was started. It had background music, and someone in a foreign accent, possibly German, was shouting out calisthenics instructions in a loud voice. "And gnow ve vill do jumping jacks! Altogether now, von-two, von-two, von-two." The idea of mass calisthenics going on with some foreign-sounding announcer was proving to be unbearable. We boys were starting to lose it.

To make matters even worse, we saw the Sisters themselves begin to perform the jumping jacks, and we couldn't contain ourselves any longer. We went hysterical. I am sure they were trying to promote leadership of this new concept by example. But we just didn't know how to handle witnessing something so out of character. Several of the boys started to laugh uncontrollably. The seventh-grade boys were doing jumping jacks completely out of rhythm to the music and directly opposed to the directions from Hans, the announcer on the record.

Then from out of the blue, it dawned on us—*Sister Bertha isn't here!* She was our teacher for the seventh grade. As I mentioned before, she was by far the toughest of all the nuns. You didn't mess with Sister Bertha, Big Bad Bertha.

For some mysterious reason, Sister Bertha was nowhere to be found. We scoured the grounds with our eyes to validate that we were left unattended, so to speak. Could it be that our actions were hidden from her sight?

With the realization that we were free to cause havoc, chaos was about to be unleashed. Before long we had a runaway. For some reason, Wally was running alongside a huge twenty-foot-high chain-link fence that stretched about ninety feet along the far east side of the playground.

All the boys in our class stopped the exercise routine, turned around, and picked up rocks. We began rapid firing at Wally, who was about sixty feet away from us. Wally was running for his life. He looked like a human duck at a shooting gallery. He kept running back and forth along the fence. We could hear the pinging of the rocks, narrowly missing his head and body, bouncing off the steel chain-link fence behind him. This was one of the funniest sights most of us had seen in our school days. By now, all of the boys were barrel laughing. Not one of the seventh-grade boys paid any attention to the instructions.

This proved so disruptive that the entire playground stopped doing the jumping jacks and other exercises.

Chaos had broken out like never before. The Sisters were shouting at us to get back in line, while the record kept blaring. The boys in our class were all over the playground, running wild, chasing Wally who had miraculously avoided the modern-day stoning. The nuns were still hysterical over the shooting gallery scene as the calisthenics class experiment proved to be one utter disaster. We didn't know it at the time, but we ourselves were heading down the road to destruction.

The bell rang to bring order to the chaos. We still couldn't contain ourselves as we made our way into a neatly formed line as we were accustomed to doing. The best thing about this was that Sister Bertha missed it all. She didn't see a thing! How unbelievable it was that none of the other Sisters seemed to be concerned about disciplining us for that bedlam on the playground. The thought of anyone watching seemed to elude us.

Boy, did we think wrong!

Little did we know, but while we were destroying the first and last physical fitness class in St. John's school history, Sister Bertha saw the whole affair from inside her window upstairs in the convent—the same convent that faced the playground. And worse yet, we had no one to defend us for our actions.

We had no idea why Sister Bertha did not accompany us out on the playground that day. We had no idea why Sister Bertha decided to stay in the convent during that time. We had no idea why Sister Bertha didn't rush out to the playground to stop the disaster. We had no idea how mad Sister Bertha could really get. But we found out one of those things for certain, because she was waiting for us back in the classroom.

I don't know whether you have ever witnessed a

mass beating in a grade school. But if I were a betting man, I would have bet that what was about to ensue would go down as one of the largest mass destructive punishments in the history of the Catholic grade school system. I had never seen Sister Bertha's face so red. I had never seen her eyes glare the way they did that afternoon. Her punishment was going to be severe, I knew that.

After bellowing that she had never seen such deplorable behavior and how ashamed she was of us, she told us that each boy in the class was going to be punished. She went on to tell us that just because she wasn't in eyesight didn't mean that she did not know what was going on. I may not have understood that before she said it, but I surely understood it at that moment.

Sister Bertha then proceeded to call each boy out into the hallway, one by one. She whaled on them one by one, blow by blow. Her wrath was unceasing. She had more than twenty-five boys to deal with on this matter. There was dead silence in the classroom while she was out in the hallway dealing the blows.

Fortunately for some of us, Sister Bertha was up in years, and her stamina began to fade as she got to about the fifteenth boy. Her face was still red; her scolding could still be heard through the walls in the classroom, but the noise was becoming less vigorous. She physically ran out of strength after the next few victims. In order to try to be just in her punishment, she made the rest of us kneel on the hardwood floors for the remaining two and a half hours in the afternoon. I knelt.

Strange things happen to us when we kneel.

I'll never forget that day. Although this story is about a day back in the early 1960s, in a way it is a typical day for many of us.

We tend to operate our lives as if God were not looking. We often make the presumption that we will not have to give an account for what we do. After all, we live in a free country, in a free society, and have the right to choose. We choose our spouses, we choose our jobs, we choose our neighborhoods, we choose our homes, we choose our political leaders. We seem to be free to choose.

We can choose; but are we free?

Before we went out on the playground that day, we were not free to cause havoc, even though we did. We instead were bound by the laws and regulations of the school to obey the instructions of the Sisters. Our freedom ended where the law began. We were free to follow the instructions. We were free to keep things orderly. We were free to start exercising when told to and stop when instructed. That is the freedom we had.

However, we violated that freedom. Why? Because something inside of us was exerting control to break the regulations. It was not a case of "The devil made me do it." It was personal; we were responsible. As we were going through the destruction of the physical fitness class, the last thing on our mind was, *What about Sister Bertha? What consequences will this bring?* The power of our sinful desires overruled any rationality or conscience. Our sinful desires had more influence on our behavior than our reason did.

This is how many of our lives are led. We live a life that we think is secret. We seldom think about the consequences, especially if they are not immediate. We conduct our lives wrongfully thinking that God Almighty does not see us, or even worse, if He does see us that it does not matter to Him. Surely, we think, He only cares about the really serious law violators such as the murderers and rapists. This is foolish thinking. It demonstrates a lack of understanding of the person of God Himself. This is a sign that there is no personal relationship, no love.

We tend to hide from God. We hide behind the thought that God will look the other way when it comes time for our account. We hide behind religion. We hope to have just enough of it to appease this God. Such thinking demonstrates that we are misled, deceived.

According to the apostle Paul, we humans live our lives according to one of two ways. These two ways are opposed to each other. The first way he called living "according to the sinful nature." The second way he called living "according to the Spirit." There's that third person of the Trinity again. Did you ever think of the *need* to live your life through the power and influence of the Holy Spirit of God?

I have some startling news for you. We are told by Paul that unless we live our lives through this second way, according to the Spirit, then we will stand before God without a defender! We will stand before the holy, almighty God, who knows and sees all things, who knows all motives behind our actions. We will indeed die in our sins, without a defender. Jesus told the Pharisees who were relying on their outward religion to appease God, "I told you that you would die in your sins; if you do not believe that I am the one I claim to be, you will indeed die in your sins" (John 8:24).

Here we are back to dealing with the Trinity again. We have a God we must stand in front of someday. Just as Sister Bertha looked out the convent window and saw us even when we didn't see her, God observes us each day at all times. This God knows the words in our mind before they are on our tongue. This God knows each and every secret motive of our hearts. This God is a supreme Judge, without error, perfectly just. God, because of His holy nature, cannot wink at our sin.

Then we have the Savior, His Son. Jesus called people to put their trust, their total trust, for their lives *in Him*. He told people that He was the way, the only way to God. He was the light for their paths. He was the truth, the revelation of God Himself in the flesh. Salvation can be found in no other. Bold claims!

Now we have the Spirit of God. The Spirit gives life to the dead. The Spirit reveals the Son of God to man. The Spirit empowers us to live like Jesus. He calls us from darkness into light. He calls us to abandon our old lives and to live out a new life, like a new creation.

This is God, working as three, but One Being—the God of history reaching out to touch man.

We must not be fooled or deceived. God does indeed watch our lives. But the good news is that He has made a new life available to you and to me. This is God's way of rescuing us from ourselves. It is also God's way of rescuing us from His wrath to come, His eternal condemnation. Unlike Sister Bertha, God will not run out of strength to punish the unjust.

Are you trying to appease God with your own morality, your religion, your own goodness? Maybe you are trying without much success. Maybe you are frustrated because the harder you try, the worse it gets. Possibly, you feel far from God and are sensing a need to be made clean. Maybe, just maybe, you are starting to understand the powerful control of our sinful nature.

No one, not one, will ever justify himself before a holy God by relying on his own efforts through a religious system. You can attend a thousand religious services and be devoted to the laws of the Church, but these in themselves will not make you right before God. You cannot add your own goodness to what God has already done on the cross. You cannot justify yourself before God, no matter how good or moral you try to become. You and I, with certainty, will fail.

Instead we must rely on One who has fully kept the Law, without a blemish, and was sacrificed as a perfect Lamb. We need to exchange our imperfect, sinful lives for His perfect, sinless life and His death in our place.

Listen to what the apostle Paul told the Romans: "Those controlled by the sinful nature cannot please God. . . . And if anyone does not have the Spirit of Christ, he does not belong to Christ" (Romans 8:8–9).

Coming to know God is a matter of meeting Him at the Cross on our knees. Knowing God is not a matter of who does the best to comply with a complex religious system. It is a matter of surrendering our nature. It is surrendering our very selves to Him who can save us.

We need to approach God with a childlike trust that Jesus is the person He claimed to be, that He is God but also a person who gave His life in exchange for ours, a perfect life for a sinful one. We need to cling with our hearts to the promise that he who believes in Christ will have eternal life. Jesus took the blows on the cross not to make Him holy, but to set us free. He suffered death on the cross so that we may be set free from the sinful nature that enslaves us. He died so that we may be set free to love His Father. His work is finished.

Now we must give up our old life and exchange it for a new one—a life in Christ, a new life born of the Spirit, a gift from God.

Jesus is the One we need to save us from the wrath of God. He is the only way that we can be reconciled to this holy God. He is the One who must stand in our place before God. It is *His* righteous life that will *justify you and me* before God. If you stand before God with your own sinful life, you will fall short, way short.

Many people are on the wrong road. The road that leads to their destruction is wide. The road that leads to life is narrow, and few find it. Although this path is narrow, there is a way to meet Him. On our knees! Strange things begin to happen to us on our knees.

When I knelt in class that day, I knelt as a punishment for my wrongdoing. But God wants us to kneel before Him out of sorrow for our sins. He wants us to kneel before Him because we realize that we are in need of Him. If I can impart any truth to you let it be this: God loves a broken and contrite heart.

I want you to read the next few chapters about a man who found a new life in Jesus while on his knees!

Chapter Eleven

MOVING
GOD TO THE
SIDELINES

My Catholic education ended with my grade school graduation. After that, I attended the local public high school, Thornton Township. I chose not to attend the Catholic high school or the seminary prep school that was available for those who wanted to become priests. I did not have "the call" to pursue a religious vocation. None of the boys from my class had the desire either. The thought of becoming a priest, and never marrying, was not exactly on top of our aspiration list.

During the high school years, I made many new friends and remained close to a few friends from grade school. I did enough to qualify for entrance into college, but I never seemed motivated to excel in academics. Competing in baseball and gymnastics was much more enticing to me at the time.

However, my life was at a crisis during the end of my final year in grade school and the first year in high school. That year my parents divorced. I do not remember much of the details, but I do remember the pain of not living with both my father and mother as I had for the first thirteen years of my life. All of a sudden, I felt that I was less important in the eyes of my parents. Their love for me, I felt, was tarnished.

For some reason my mother, my older sister, Sue, and I moved out of our house into an apartment across town. My older brother, Ben, was twenty-one and finishing his tour in the Navy. I missed my old bedroom. I missed the parts of the house that I had used for a makeshift basketball court. My security had been shaken to its roots. I longed for us to be together as a family as we once were.

Little did I know that God's hand was upon me. Even though I did not know Him or truly love Him, He loved me. By the grace of God the divorce lasted only about a year and a half. My mother and father were reunited in marriage, and we moved back to our old modest house. I do not remember ever discussing this whole ordeal with anyone in those days. In that era it was just understood that marriage was for a lifetime. It was believed to be right for the family to be together, and it was believed to be wrong to be separated by divorce.

I wasn't religious among my high school friends, nor was I irreligious. Many of my friends were non-Catholic. At the public high school I was exposed to people from various backgrounds and religions. We never talked about religion that I can remember. Yet I was very much Catholic and knew no other way to God. I needed to make myself right for God to accept me. It was what I had been taught in those eight years of rigorous catechism training.

During my sophomore year in high school, after my parents remarried, my outlook on life was much brighter. Things were about to get even brighter as I was destined to know Noreen, the girl of my dreams, who later would be my life partner.

I still remember the day that I first saw her in my Spanish II class when I was a junior and she was a sophomore. Noreen had an attractive, outgoing personality and cute features. Her gentle spirit caught my attention—as did her blonde hair, blue eyes, and petite figure. Over time, I came to admire her sincerity and her deep and profound sense of love for others, particularly people in need. We met in 1966 and have been together ever since.

She had just transferred to our public high school from the Catholic high school in a nearby community. She lived directly across the street from our high school, which she had wanted to attend in the first place. Instead, Noreen took the bus each day for a twenty-five-minute commute to and from her school until she transferred to the public school.

Noreen had attended and graduated from the Ascension Catholic grade school, which was located on the opposite side of our hometown of Harvey. She came from a strong sense of family. She had seven brothers and sisters; she was the sixth in line, just ahead of her younger twin brother and sister. She loved her family, and they were kind enough to make me feel very welcome in their home.

My relationship with Noreen continued to grow. By the time I was ready to move to my college town, we had been dating steadily for about a year. She had one more year of high school to complete as I went away to a whole new world.

I was seventeen years old on my way to attend a four-year university some three hundred miles from home. I was the first member from my father's side of the family to attend a higher education institution. I was preparing to attend a secular university, but I don't think I even stopped to wonder if that environment would affect the way I thought about God.

My cousin Dean was the only member of our family, on my mother's side, who had completed college. He proved to be the link I needed to help me learn the proper study habits needed to get through school. Before I left for the university, Dean wrote out a detailed list of things that were crucial to understand if I was to make it in the college world. There would be no more teachers willing to hold my hand. If I did not do the work, there were no notes home to my parents. I would be expected to read the material, attend the lectures, study my notes, and spit back the knowledge on the exams. If it wasn't for the methodical advice outlining how one should study and review the class material, I would have likely gone down as another college statistical dropout. I am grateful that God knew my shortcomings and apparently had other plans for me.

My college years went by quickly. Noreen transferred to the university during my junior year, her sophomore year in 1970. We were both twenty years old. Both of us knew that marriage was definitely in the future.

We both still attended Mass regularly each Sunday through the local Catholic Newman Center at the University. Although we did not attend on the Holy Days of Obligation any longer, we usually received communion each Sunday. But for me the Newman Center was only a place to fulfill our weekly obligation, nothing more. My view was that the Church was there to provide the avenue to stay out of mortal sin. The Church was the place to receive Holy Communion, which should help me in some way to make myself right before God.

If I were to be honest with myself, I would have admitted that I did not enjoy going to Mass each week. I would have admitted that the reason I went was that it was obligatory under punishment of mortal sin if I willfully missed. I received communion, but again, if I were honest, I would have had to admit that I did so because this was expected of me as a Catholic or that somehow receiving communion was contributing to my salvation. The best way I can put it is that I relied on the Catholic Church to be my salvation, but it didn't affect my life much.

College students are, by design, exposed to various philosophies. Although I was not greatly affected by any one philosopher or philosophy, there seemed to be little, if any, discussion about God. We were taught to cherish our reason. We were given courses in logic, philosophy, art, environment, and anthropology. The humanities curriculum was obviously man-centered and had no integration with the being of God. This was the early 1970s, the era when *Time* magazine pronounced that God was dead.

Little did I know that I was being desensitized to the things of God. I never heard the word *creation* in a science course. I never heard the words *sin* or *damnation* in an anthropology class. Science, sociology, anthropology, and philosophy were presenting new worldviews for me. I was slowly being exposed to a whole new world that did not contain or seem to need God.

But this learning would bring me worldly success. I was confident by my junior year that I could master this college system. I could do as well as anyone in my classes if I just put my mind to it. I was an average student in high school, but now I was pulling down A's and B's in subjects like physics, calculus, and advanced statistics. If I liked the subject matter, I usually excelled in the class.

Mathematics had always been my strong suit. I decided in high school that I wanted to become a certified public accountant. Thus I pursued accounting as my major. I didn't know any accountants. I had never done any real accounting work other than what we worked on in my two high school bookkeeping classes. But this seemed to be a good choice since I was proficient in mathematics.

I did OK in my main accounting courses, but I certainly didn't love them. I did OK in the other business disciplines such as marketing, economics, and management, but I certainly didn't love them. At the end of my junior year, one year away from graduation, I had two solid years of courses in my major behind me, but I wasn't crazy about this academic discipline as a future career.

My father-in-law-to-be was a banker at the First National Bank in Harvey. He knew several businessmen around the town. Two contacts he had were partners in a small, local CPA firm. He asked them if his daughter's boyfriend could work there in the summer of 1971 as an intern. They agreed, and before I knew it, I was working as an auditor for this local firm. Finally, I would get a real taste of what real accountants do for a living.

It was a little intimidating for me. The work was tedious, and at times it was over my head. I couldn't seem to grasp the big picture. I knew what I was doing, but I didn't know why I was doing it. There was little hands-on training. Interns were supposed to just know how to do the things that needed to be done, and the other interns seemed to grasp it better than I did.

At the end of the summer, the firm gave a test to all of its half-dozen interns. The partners of the firm were testing to see how well we grasped the auditing/accounting profession. It was somewhat of a screening device to see who would make a good accountant for them someday. I took the test with great fear, believing that this test would flush out my true feelings and skills. I was right.

One partner went over the results with me. He was very candid. He suggested that maybe, based on how I scored on the test, I should look seriously at another profession. I was devastated by the results and his summarization of my career as an aspiring accountant.

I had one year left to complete my bachelor's degree in accounting, and I did not want to give up on all that I had accomplished up until that point. I took an elective course on teaching methods from the education department. The course was designed for those who wanted to teach business subjects to high school students.

I loved the course. I began to investigate what it would take to pick up a bachelor's degree in business teacher education so that someday I could teach high school. I was in luck: Because of all the business courses I had already completed with my accounting degree, I only had to take a few education and teaching method courses and then student-teach for one quarter. If I pushed myself, I could complete this all with only one additional year of school.

I graduated in 1972 with my bachelor's degree in accounting. Noreen had one more year to complete her bachelor's degree in elementary education. It would work out well. Since Noreen had to come back for one more year to finish her degree, I could return to school and finish the necessary requirements to become a certified teacher.

I was well on my way to a life in which God played the role of an extra.

Chapter Twelve

I WAS
EMPTY

Noreen and I married in the summer of 1972. After five years of serious dating, we tied the knot. Kenny, my first college roommate and friend from grade school and high school, was our best man. Noreen and I were now one. Things were going great. After I married my high school sweetheart, we moved into our own first apartment back down at school in the fall. We were finishing school together, and we were in love in our own little world. It really seemed as though life would be "happily ever after."

After graduation in the summer of 1973, we made our way back home. We found an apartment in the south suburbs of Chicago in a town called Tinley Park. I landed a teaching job at a local high school in the business education department. Noreen secured a teacher's aide position at a local elementary school.

We continued to practice our Catholic faith. We attended Mass each Sunday at our local Catholic parish. We continued to receive the sacrament of Communion. Confessions to the priest were rare, but within the statutory limits of at least once per year. We never discussed religion much among our family. There just never seemed a need to discuss God except in the most casual way.

I was teaching business education subjects such as accounting, business law, and data processing. I was helping to coach the two same sports I participated in during my high school days, baseball and gymnastics. I was teaching mostly junior and senior students, and I loved what I was doing. From all human reason, I should not have been wanting, but I began to grow restless in life. I was growing discontent with the limited potential for my future—the potential for a higher standard of living, that is.

In the summer during my teaching years, I went to work for the CPA firm that I had worked for in the summer of 1971. Noreen by now had secured a full-time teaching position at her school. Our income was pretty decent for those days. We were starting to enjoy the things in life that two incomes made possible.

We purchased our first home in the summer of 1975 after two years of apartment living. We skimped and saved, and with a generous contribution to our down payment from my parents, we bought our first home. A large investment with a large mortgage greatly influenced what I needed to do with my career.

When we had been married for almost five years, Noreen found out that she was expecting our first child. Although I cherished the notion of being a father, this meant that her paychecks were soon to be a thing of the past. Noreen was very intent on staying home and giving up her teaching position when we had a baby. The CPA firm that I worked for in the summers wanted me to consider joining them on a full-time basis. This was a very difficult decision for me. I loved my teaching and coaching responsibilities, but I knew that I wanted to do more. I wanted to be able to continue to afford the nice things in life, to become a financial success. I didn't see that happening on my teacher's salary.

After struggling with the idea, I decided to leave my teaching position. I was convinced that if I could pass the CPA exam, then the doors would be flung open for me to achieve great success. I accepted a full-time position with the accounting firm in the summer of 1977. The firm would also pay all my expenses to prepare and sit for the CPA exam.

I was deep along the path. I was looking for that something to provide deep-seated happiness. I was looking for something to give me joy. I was trying to satisfy my desires with the solutions that the world offered. I did not know at this time just how dangerous this wrong road was going to get.

On March 30, 1978, our daughter, Erin Maureen, was brought into our world for us to love and to care for. Her name is very Irish, to be sure. Since we had very little Irish heritage between us, the name sounded foreign, but it was a perfect name, for her hair was beautifully red and her eyes were deep blue. She was an Erin if I had ever seen one. God had blessed us with a beautiful child.

My next goal in life was to pass the CPA exam. The firm was counting on me to achieve this distinction. To advance in the world of accounting it is usually necessary for one to get these three initials behind one's name as soon as possible. I had heard horror stories about the difficulty of the exam, and it had been more than six years since I had taken my last accounting course. But I knew that it was more than just passing an exam: It was my ticket to happiness. I had given up my teaching career, which I loved, for a career that I didn't love. But if I could just get those initials behind my name, then my life would be fulfilled. If I could achieve this one feat, then my life would be met with much success and happiness.

The exam I was preparing for was being offered in Chicago in May of 1978. Three months prior to the exam I enrolled in an intensive review course that met for four hours two times a week. The homework assignments from this course, coupled with the studying for the exam, was intense.

During the month of April prior to the exam, I committed to study eight hours on Saturday and the same on Sunday along with my regular review course during the week. I was bound and determined to pass the exam, even though only about 10 to 15 percent of the candidates pass the exam on their first try.

I needed to pass at least two of the four parts of the exam in order to keep them as credit for the whole. If I passed only one part, I would lose it and it would be necessary to sit for the entire four parts of the exam again.

I had many of the things that I desired. I had a lovely wife, the wife of my youth. I had a beautiful little red-haired daughter that I thanked God for. We were only twenty-seven years old, and we had been in our own house for three years already. I had a very good professional job, which provided a decent salary. We lived in a wonderful community with country charm. I had good health. I had it all; but I was empty. I waited eagerly for my grades to come back, because I believed that would change my life and finally leave me fulfilled.

My grades came back from New York in August. I

had heard that if I passed the exam, my envelope would be a little thicker because it would contain material for me to join the various state and national CPA organizations. Since I didn't have a barometer to measure the thickness, I just hoped those pamphlets were in the envelope.

I held my breath and opened the envelope. My heart sank as I read the scores. I had passed only one of the four sections required. That meant I would have to sit for the entire, grueling three-day exam once again. I would have to study intensely all over again.

Although I was extremely disappointed, there was a silver lining. My actual scores were very close to passing. I was only a few points away from passing each part. That gave me a sense of hope.

I decided to go at it again right away. So I applied for the next available exam, which was in November of 1978. I had saved all of my review materials, and I was now more determined than ever to pass.

The months flew by quickly. I was engrossed in my work, but not enjoying it. I decided to devote the entire month of October to once again study for the exam. So after work each day and on the weekends I went over the material again and again. My goal was to study approximately forty hours a week for four weeks straight. I pored over former exam questions night after night.

I remember Noreen putting my meals on a tray outside the door of my room on the weekends. I didn't see much of Noreen or Erin during that month. I was committed to passing that exam.

The exam came and went. It was just as tough as the last one. However, a long problem in the exam dealt with an area of my own specialty. I was sure I did well on that major question and I hoped I impressed the examiners. I had to wait until January, some three months, for the results to come.

I pictured that if I did pass the exam, I would run outside and jump up and down on my car. I was hoping, with all my heart, that I could get those three initials behind my name. I had had that dream ever since my high school days some eleven years before.

On a cold January day Noreen called me at the office of a client that I was working with at the time. She said my grades had come in the mail. I asked her not to open the envelope, because I wanted the joy of victory or the agony of defeat to be mine. It was a long ride home that night from the city of Chicago to the southwest suburb of Frankfort. The thought of opening that envelope was agonizing. I had a million different scenarios going through my mind on that drive home.

I raced into the house and found the envelope waiting for me. My wife and daughter were in the family room with me as I once again held my breath. But one thing seemed different. This envelope felt thicker than the last one!

When I realized this, I tore open the envelope and quickly zeroed in on the grades. I had passed all four parts of the exam. It was over; I did it. I was now a CPA!

I had now been given the key to happiness and joy. But the strangest thing happened. I didn't have the urge to go out and jump up and down on my car. Finally, I had achieved what I worked so hard for. I was excited, but it was not at all what I expected the feeling to be. A profound sense of emptiness flooded my soul.

Chapter Thirteen

MY SCARLET LETTER

Soon after I passed the CPA exam I began searching for the next avenue to success and happiness. For various reasons, I decided to resign from my position as an audit supervisor of the public accounting firm to wind up in the private world of business.

My dissatisfaction of working in public accounting was increasing. The deep fulfillment from passing the CPA exam never materialized. Noreen was happy being a mother and homemaker and immensely enjoying our new daughter Erin. But I felt that something was missing. It was time to look for that success, time to fulfill that emptiness in my heart.

I rashly quit my job at the accounting firm before I secured another position. I was tired of the politics and the lack of fulfilling work. But I had a wife, a child, a large mortgage, and two automobiles to support.

I found a search firm in Chicago that helped place accountants/auditors with companies in the Chicagoland area for a fee. Best of all, the company that did the hiring paid the fee. To my amazement I had two job offers three weeks into my search. I weighed the offers and decided against the travel commitment that I would have to make at one company. I accepted the position of senior auditor at the other company.

Seeking to enhance my chances of advancement within the company, I immediately began planning how I could master the system that would lead to happiness. I figured that the CPA status was helpful, but having an MBA (master of business administration) would be a sure ticket.

In January of 1980, I enrolled at a local university and began to pursue my MBA degree. Within two years, I was promoted from the auditing department to a higher-level position in the finance division. The company had created a new position for me that would entail automating the entire company's accounting system. Not bad, I thought, for a guy who was told ten years previously that he should consider another field than accounting.

My new job was at the largest company and/or entity that I had ever been exposed to. I was becoming very confident in my work and myself. I was progressing faster than most in the company. I was quickly gaining the respect of the senior management.

Our second child was born in February 1981—Ryan Michael, our first son. I couldn't have been prouder of this blond-haired, blue-eyed delight. God had now given us two beautiful children. Ryan was the son every father would die for: all boy, athletic, with a deep voice from childhood.

My beliefs about God had not changed much since my youth. A deep sense of right and wrong was embedded into my conscience from my Catholic upbringing. We still attended Mass each Sunday as a family. I was even asked to be on the parish board of our local Catholic Church. I served on the board for two years. Things were going well, it seemed to me.

I graduated from Lewis University with my MBA degree in June of 1983, and my future at my company looked very bright. In fact, the next year I was promoted to an executive position that had responsibility of the Financial Planning and Systems Development for the entire company. This was a visible and lofty position in the company, and I was entering it at the young age of thirty-three.

In 1984 our second son, Mark Richard, was born. He was precious in my sight, and we were now a family of five. Mark brought with him a gentle spirit and a loving, sensitive manner, and he is very bright.

However, something less attractive entered my life during this time—something that went against all that I knew to be right. It started innocently enough. In 1981, at the age of thirty, I yearned to get back into sports. I received much satisfaction from participating and coaching. I played semiprofessional baseball in my mid-twenties and participated in a softball league after that. But when I received a concussion playing softball one evening, my desire to play competitive baseball diminished.

Volleyball was just beginning to become popular with adults in the early 1980s. It was a new sport for me, but I picked it up with zeal. I started to play on a volleyball league through the local park district one night a week. It was another avenue to look for the deep satisfaction my soul yearned for. God was going to show me that no one and no thing could give me the joy and peace I was looking for.

Volleyball was a new thing for me to master. It was a

team sport that took the involvement of all six players to be successful. Unfortunately for me, half of the players were of the opposite sex. It was the first time I ever engaged in competitive sports with women on the same team. This scenario would prove to be a fatal attraction. I was coming into the final stretch of the wide road that was leading slowly to my destruction.

During 1981, Noreen started to become, in my eyes, ever more religious. Not religious in the sense of going to Mass more, saying the rosary, or lighting vigil candles. But she started saying prayers with our children before bedtime and doing something that I had never seen her do: reading and studying the Bible. She even joined a group of women who intently studied the Bible. Over time this change was becoming more pronounced. Something was different about her. I could not put my finger on it, but I saw more and more of a changed person. Noreen seemed to integrate God more into our everyday life. She referred to God more and talked freely about Him. I certainly believed in God, but she talked about Him as if she knew Him personally.

Since the days of my youth, I always wanted to know how things were processed, what made them work. I needed to know the system. I don't mean mechanically; for me it was always needing to know how abstract things could be made known. I guess that is why my desires were really in teaching.

This need transferred into the religious realm. Ever since I was young, I had tried to understand the system taught by the Catholic Catechism. Religiously, I needed to understand how to make myself right before God. God was about to reveal the truth about Himself and myself in a most profound way.

Around 1984, two major events began to unravel in my life. Shortly after my promotion, a bigger position opened due to a resignation. This new opening was the controller's job, a position that most accountants aspire to as a significant recognition of their accounting acumen and management skills. Since I never could seem to find contentment in what I had already accomplished, I pursued this new position with zeal. After all, I was in control.

I felt sincerely, possibly naively, that it was very likely that I would be named to this position. Although not the most experienced, I was the most qualified academically. I felt that I was the right fast-track person, at the right time for this opening. I made my intentions known to the vice president of finance, to which this position reported. Although he did not say no, he didn't seem overly excited about my being a prospect. But in my mind, I was the most logical choice. One of my co-workers even came into my office and congratulated me, for he was sure that I was going be awarded the position.

Two weeks later I was being introduced to the new controller, who was someone hired from the outside with an MBA and a CPA behind his name. He was older, more experienced, and came from a larger international company where he had served as an assistant controller. It made sense to them, but not to me. I felt betrayed. I went through all this effort to get myself in position to qualify for the job, and they gave it to an outsider. When I later asked about the reason for my not getting the position, I was told that I was just too young. Although they were probably right, there was no way I was going to concede to their logic at that point in my life. My life started to go into a tailspin after that.

During the same time period my volleyball prowess was increasing. I was becoming enthralled with playing. I lived to play on Wednesday nights. However, there was one major problem developing: I was starting to form a relationship with one of the women on the team who was also married.

My bitterness grew toward my company and in particular toward my new boss who was given the controller's throne. I despised coming to work for him each day, since I believed it was he who took away my hope of happiness. This was compounded by the fact that his people skills were often mean-spirited and self-glorifying. He was smothering me. I didn't believe I needed his help, and I certainly didn't need his criticism at every turn.

I was looking for that one relationship, that one promotion, that one advanced degree, that one something to bring me happiness, to bring joy and peace to my life. God was allowing me to be filled with myself, and it wasn't satisfying. My marriage was beginning to crumble. I became very distant from my family.

The scene started to get ugly, for my addiction turned from volleyball to adultery. I was now involved in a relationship that had started out innocently enough around a game, but had turned into a secret affair. Our volleyball matches inevitably carried over to the local tavern where we rehashed the night over drinks. It started with a few drinks and the night ending around 11:00 P.M. It evolved to many drinks and coming home at 2:00 A.M.

I remember coming home later and later, sometimes not even remembering how I drove home. Our children were always in bed, so they never saw me in this condition. I can distinctly remember coming home very late, my heart filled with guilt over what I was doing. As I came into the house, I would take our family picture down off our fireplace mantel and stare at it. Tears often rolled down my cheeks onto the picture itself. I knew what I was doing was wrong. Even though my conscience said this was wrong, a more powerful part of me said it didn't matter. I did not seem to have the power to free myself of this fatal attraction. Who could help me?

This was causing havoc in our family, most notably in my relationship with the wife of my youth. Although Noreen was not aware of an actual affair going on, she was not blind to my behavior. One of the worst dilemmas for me was that I knew I was hurting Noreen, yet I couldn't seem to muster the strength or willpower to stop what I was doing. Noreen is a very sensitive woman, and to her the thought of me being with someone else just couldn't be true.

Through her tears she often said to me, "You need to be born again!" I scoffed at such a statement. I didn't particularly care for those folks who considered themselves to be born-again Christians. I especially didn't appreciate those who I referred to as "Bible thumpers."

I asked her, "What do you mean, be born again? Why would I need to be born again? I never died!" My words rang with a truth that at the time I could not imagine. It was certainly true; I had never died to myself.

I felt as if I were sinking into a deep hole, one that I seemed to have no power to pull myself from. My life was becoming unraveled, and the knowledge of doing something that would condemn my soul to hell was causing me tremendous anxiety.

Meanwhile, my intense dislike for my new boss drove me to a major career decision. I was prepared to leave the company or be transferred to a new department away from him. I prayed that God would help me make the right decision. Even though I was in deep sin, somehow I felt that God would and could help me.

During this time, I made my feelings known to the manager of human resources, who happened to be a friend of mine. Bob Thayer had earlier taught with me at the same high school. Bob's wife, Judy, had been a classmate with Noreen and me in high school. Bob said that he would talk it over with his boss, who was the same person who had hired me into the company five years earlier.

He got back to me with an answer that I was glad to hear. I could move into a company position in the human resources department. It would mean a lateral job transfer. This was good, but it also meant that my finance fast-tracking career was likely finished. Although I hesitated to take the position because of that, the alternative of leaving the company I liked was not very appealing.

The division transfer was made. I was branded with a scarlet letter "A" from the finance division. Now I was carrying two scarlet letters with me. I had made the decision to leave my division. My affair with the other woman was deepening. I was now coming to a decision as to my beloved wife.

Chapter Fourteen

TRYING TO STAY IN CONTROL

I accepted the new position in human resources, commonly known in those days as the personnel department. My new responsibilities entailed the management of the employee benefit plans of the company. I didn't know much about this particular function. What I did know was that I inherited a mess. This position had been without a manager for six months, and the work to be done was tremendous.

But although I was totally off the track that I wanted to pursue, I did gain one thing by the move: I now reported to a higher-level person, a vice president of the company. This reporting relationship carried with it a certain status level of its own.

My new boss, Harold Dahlstrand, was a hands-off kind of executive who didn't seem to have a chip on his shoulder. I didn't sense that he was out to punish me if I failed. We developed an excellent business relationship and a personal friendship as well. I was starting to enjoy myself at work again.

However, the volleyball league continued and the

nights out at the bars increased. Noreen and I were now inevitably moving toward the end of our fourteen-year marriage. My heart was ever so slowly becoming hardened to Noreen. Both of us had many nights of tears as I continued to come home in the wee hours of the morning. Many nights I came home late intoxicated and collapsed in the bed, only to get up and put in a full day at the office on three or four hours sleep.

I was able to hide the reality of things quite well from my co-workers, family, and friends. I could hide it every way possible, except one. I knew that I was not hiding this from God. I knew that He could see all that was going on. I knew that I was in jeopardy of spending my eternity in hell, because what I was doing was clearly a mortal sin. My behavior was a blatant breaking of the commandment of God.

I tried to confess this to a priest, but somehow I couldn't get the courage to do it. I was in a terrible dilemma, because I believed this was the only way my grievous sin could be forgiven. I anguished over what was happening. I was torn over the pain that I was causing Noreen. Deep down in my heart I did not want to end our marriage. I did not want my children to go through the anguish that I experienced as a child. The pain from my parents' divorce brought back too many unpleasant memories for me. Somehow in God's profound wisdom, He had allowed me to experience that pain as a child.

To put it simply, I was miserable. My dear father, who had died in 1980, was not there to see the guilt, the shame. My mother asked Noreen what was wrong with me, because I seemed so withdrawn. I remember sitting by myself outside on our patio while the family was inside. My mother could see in my eyes that something was terribly wrong.

My mother sensed that our marriage was in deep trouble. One day, she said something to me that pierced my heart. She said, "If your marriage ends, and the two of you are separated, then I wish I would have died with your father." Our situation complicated her pain since she had to endure the divorces of my brother and sister as well. I couldn't stop the feeling of being dragged into this sinkhole.

The situation was extremely frustrating for me, for I had always been in control of my life. If I wanted something badly enough I just exerted the needed strength, knowledge, and willpower to get it. That was the story of my life. But this was somehow beyond me. This sinful desire seemed to be more powerful than my will to stop. Somehow, I felt helpless. I longed for the willpower to stop. The thought of my beautiful family being destroyed was tearing me up.

I can remember driving to work one morning and crying out at the top of my lungs, "Somebody help me; please, somebody help me!"

It is difficult to portray the depravity of the soul with words. The closest similarity would be someone who is addicted to alcohol or drugs. Intellectually the person knows it is wrong, intellectually he knows he should stop, but the desires of the sinful nature are too powerful to contain. The phrase, "the spirit is willing but the flesh is weak" certainly could have applied in my case. By September 1986 our marriage was deteriorating rapidly.

Noreen decided that she wanted to attend a different church. The church she wanted to attend was not a Catholic church, but a church that one of our neighbors attended. Noreen asked if she could start going there and take the children also. A few years before, I would have never agreed. But I didn't seem to care about these things anymore. Instead of saying absolutely not, I found myself bargaining with her.

As absurd as this may sound, I negotiated that if she wanted to leave the Catholic Church, then I would play volleyball one additional night a week. Although she was reluctant, Noreen agreed to the pact. I was being consumed by my concern for my own wants. I wanted to have my own desires met, no matter how sinful they may have been.

The next three months went from bad to worse. Although I didn't know it at the time, Noreen began to seek counsel from the pastor at her new church regarding our marriage. She continued to attend her new church, and I continued to attend at the old parish. As much as I disliked Noreen's involvement in this Bible study and her attending a church that was not Catholic, I could not deny the positive changes that I saw in her. But I was putting some or much of the blame of our marriage problems on Noreen for her heightened interest in religious things. Her vigor for her beliefs became a dividing wedge in our marriage. Although I would not openly admit it, I sensed that Noreen was grasping onto something that gave her strength and peace through all of this.

However, after a few months went by, Noreen said that she did not want to live in this situation anymore. On Wednesday, December 3, she went in to pray and seek advice from the minister at her new church. I found out later that on that day they prayed to God that I would be delivered. Basically, they were praying for a miracle.

Meanwhile my new boss, Harold, who was not aware of the turmoil in my family life, invited me to attend a breakfast meeting to be held on Friday, December 5, 1986. These meetings for professionals and business-people in the community were held once a month at a hotel next to our office building. They normally lasted an hour and featured a motivational guest speaker. It was common to have a Fortune 500 CEO, a popular sports figure, or someone in a major leadership position. But since it was the Christmas season the speaker for Friday was different—he was a minister.

Harold, whom I considered to be religious, asked me to attend the breakfast. I was not excited about going to hear a minister speak. Something within me scoffed at the idea. What could this preacher teach me about the business world? At the same time, I believed that it would be politically unwise for me to turn down Harold's request to attend. I reasoned that not going could hamper my career, so I went. Although it was in God's eternal plan that I attend, something stirring within me tried to reason why I should not go. It seemed to be the same inner voice that was leading me to places that I should never have gone.

Although I did not know it, the end of the wide road leading to my destruction was near.

Chapter Fifteen

"DON'T YOU KNOW THAT I GAVE MY SON FOR YOU?"

It was December 5, 1986, very early Friday morning. I had to get out of bed at 5:00 A.M., an hour earlier than usual. It was the day I had to go to the breakfast meeting at the Marriott Hotel in Oakbrook, Illinois.

The featured speaker that morning was the Rev. John Guest, a minister from a church in Sewickley, Pennsylvania. A choir sang Christmas carols before he spoke. This was not the normal protocol, but of course it was the Christmas season. I looked at my watch as the speaker began, like I usually did in church, to get a sense of how long this guy was going to speak. I was hoping for a quick fifteen-minute homily, a short prayer, and then dismissal so I could get out of there.

John Guest's physical appearance and English accent both reminded me of the Beatles. It caught me by surprise that he began with a very humorous story. His voice was enjoyable to listen to with his English accent and all. He spoke about the reality of life, but he used the Beatles' music to illustrate false philosophies, and he talked about teenage suicide. He wasn't like any other preacher I had ever heard.

I really was enjoying his presentation. He was funny, he was articulate, and he seemed to be extremely insightful. When he mentioned that he only had five minutes left to conclude his remarks, I did not want him to end. I could have sat there and continued to listen to his insights into life. There was something attractive about him, not just in the physical sense, but also in his honest perspective. He seemed to exude a sense of confidence of the truth, and his joy could be witnessed on his face. He said that before he finished he wanted to leave us with a true story he had recently heard.

This is a recount of the gripping story that he told that morning.

There was a man who lived near the Mississippi River and worked in a modest job as a drawbridge operator. One day the man decided to take his young son and daughter to work with him to show them what he did on his job. He was showing them around the area, when all of a sudden he received a call on his radio that he needed to get up to the control tower room to put down the drawbridge. The train was ten minutes ahead of schedule that day. At the time, he and his children were near the room with all the dangerous heavy machinery and working gears that moved the bridge up and down. He put his two children on the railing and told them not to get down from there until he returned. He warned them of the danger and again told them not to move. He then made his way quickly up to the control tower some ten minutes away. He saw that the train was coming, and he was preparing to lower the bridge. He saw all of the people sitting on the train.

He took one more look at his children before he lowered the bridge. He was horribly shocked when he saw that his son had climbed down off the railing and had crawled among the dangerous gears. The father was caught in a terrible dilemma. If he lowered the bridge, then he would surely crush his son to death in the gears. If he didn't lower the bridge, then more than two hundred people would crash into the raised bridge. He had to make an immediate decision; the train was approaching and it would take too long to rescue his son. The father knew what he had to do.

During this story I was putting myself in the father's position. I thought to myself, *How terrible. What would I have done if that had been my son Ryan or Mark?* He continued the story.

The father then pushed the button that engaged the gears that began to lower the bridge. He witnessed his son being crushed to death. With tears in his eyes, he pounded on the glass and shouted to the people sitting on the train, "Don't you know what I have done for you? Don't you know that I gave you my only son so that you could live? I gave you my only son so that you may live!" The people on the train couldn't hear his screaming. They instead were sitting comfortably on the train reading their newspapers and drinking their coffee.

The tears were welling up in my eyes, and I was fighting them back. Something moved me on the inside. Something about his talk that morning began a stir in me. Something in this story was deeper than the story itself. I was trying to hide from the others at the table that

117

I had tears in my eyes. I was profoundly moved by this story, but I couldn't explain it.

Before I wanted it to end, the breakfast was over and we began to make our way back to the office next door. As we got out to the parking lot, I told Harold that the speaker was one of the best I had ever heard. I really meant it. Harold said, "Yeah, I thought he was going to have an altar call." I stopped and looked at him quizzically. I didn't know what that meant. I knew what an altar was, but I had never heard of an "altar call." He could tell by the look on my face that I did not know what he meant.

He looked me right in the eye and said, "That's where you go up to the front by the speaker and give your life to Christ!" I nodded, but I didn't say anything. I thought to myself, *If the minister had done that, I would have gone up.*

I told Harold that I needed to get my briefcase from my car and that I would see him later that day in the office. I went to my car to get my briefcase, and I remained in my car for the next several minutes. For some reason I began to weep. I wept hard for several minutes before I could regain my composure. I could only think about that story. I couldn't get that story out of my mind. I had never wept that deeply, but somehow I felt refreshed; for some reason, I felt new.

My friend Bob Thayer, who attended the breakfast with us, noticed that the minister's talk had an impact on me. That morning, he phoned his wife Judy, who was a friend of my wife, Noreen, to tell her of his observations. Judy called Noreen later that morning to tell her that something had happened to me as a result of the breakfast meeting.

I too called Noreen later that day, and I told her I wanted to tell her about the minister that I had heard that morning. We agreed to talk when I got home that evening. Although I didn't know it, she had already been advised about this by Judy.

Later that evening, after we got the kids into bed, I told Noreen about the minister that I had heard that morning. I told her the story about the drawbridge. I told her that I was starting to cry as I imagined myself being in the shoes of the father. She explained to me that the story was about God reaching out to man. *It was?*

"Yes," she said. "You see, the father in the tower is to be seen as God the Father. It is God the Father who gave us His Son, His one and only Son so that you can live! He sacrificed His Son Jesus on a cross so that you can live. He gives us life through the Son!" I wanted to know more.

I told her that must be why Harold had thought the minister was going to have an "altar call." I explained to her that he told me, "That's where you go up and give your life to Christ." She seemed to already know about such a thing. Giving one's life to Christ is surrendering our will and attitude to a new Master. It is relinquishing our efforts to make ourselves right before God. It is answering the call of God, to our mind and emotions, to trust in Him and in Him alone for our salvation. It is not our work, but rather trusting in His work. Noreen told me, "You can give your life to Christ right now."

I thought to myself, *Now? In the family room?* I didn't want to question it. Instead I said, "I want to do that!"

She asked me to kneel down. As I did so, she knelt beside me, placed her hands on my head, and prayed like I'd never heard prayer before. She prayed that God would forgive me for all of my sins and that I would receive a new life in God. I was praying silently from my heart for the same. I had never heard a prayer that wasn't memorized or read. Although my eyes were closed and my head bowed, her prayer was so sincere and eloquent that I thought she must have read that prayer.

When I had my head bowed and while Noreen and I were praying, I felt a tremendous load being lifted off my shoulders. Although I couldn't have verbalized what took place, I knew one thing for sure; my sins had been forgiven. The sins that I had carried with me all of my thirty-five years of life were taken away. God removed something from me that I couldn't do myself. He removed the guilt of my sins! He gave them to His Son Jesus. Jesus bore upon Himself my sins. His magnificent love for me flooded my very being. I had received the free gift of salvation from God Himself.

It was the beginning of a new life in Christ. The hunt for meaning was over; I had surrendered on my knees. I knew that my sins were forgiven. I had met a holy God. My guilt was exposed before God, and I wept for my sins.

My God had given up His Son to take on the punishment for my sinful acts; my rebellion against God was borne by Jesus. God allowed Jesus to be crushed and beaten and crucified for my sins. I now experienced the deep love that God has for us; I experienced His mercy and His grace. I was now free—free to love God and to serve Him. Jesus had set me free—free to turn from my sin and the sinful lifestyle I was living. God had given me true life, eternal life. The story that I heard that day was the answer to the prayers for me. The Gospel had the power to deliver me from my sins—the power, as God allowed me to clearly realize, that I did not have within myself.

The truth of my earlier words had now rung true: I had not been ready to be born again because I had never died. I had now died to the power of sin; I was born again, I was free.

Chapter Sixteen

THE WIDE AND NARROW ROADS

I had found it! After all those years of looking for peace and joy, I had truly found it! But the joy and happiness I had found were not in an "it"; they were in a *person*. That person was Jesus. The wide road I was traveling down had a sure outcome: It finished with a dead-end sign. It was leading to my eventual destruction in a permanent separation from God.

The happiness and joy I was ever searching for were found when I died, that is, when I surrendered my old life. I wanted life, but little did I realize that in order to have true new life, I must first die to the old one. I could now begin to understand the paradoxical teaching of Jesus when He said, "For whoever wants to save his life will lose it, but whoever loses his life for me will save it. What good is it for a man to gain the whole world, and yet lose or forfeit his very self?" (Luke 9:24–25).

That was me: I was trying to gain the whole world. I was looking to the things of this world to bring me happiness and joy. I had now found true peace and joy, and I had found them in the person of Jesus. I had tasted the water that quenches thirst. I had eaten of the bread that satisfies the pain of spiritual hunger. I knew it was real, because it filled my heart and quenched my thirst like no other. It filled the emptiness in my heart. This is what Jesus meant when He said, "Come to me, all you who are weary and burdened, and I will give you rest. Take my yoke upon you and learn from me, for I am gentle and humble in heart, and you will find rest for your souls. For my yoke is easy and my burden is light" (Matthew 11:28–30).

Up until this point, I was trying my best to make myself right with God. But according to the Bible, my sin had deceived me, because human righteousness is impossible. I had failed miserably; I had fallen far short. I was trying to fill my life with the things of this world that seemed to be able to bring me true happiness and true joy. But the things of this world can never satisfy the soul, for the soul is eternal and this world is temporary. The soul must be satisfied by something that is eternal, something that transcends our own being. My wanting only led to despair. It wasn't until that day that I experienced the truth, that my spirit was made alive! God tells us we are a people who need to believe in the truth of the Gospel. We need to embrace God's grace through the good news of Jesus Christ.

This is exactly what Jesus was telling Nicodemus. This is exactly what my precious wife, Noreen, was trying to tell me. I needed to be born again; I needed to receive the new life that only God can give. But first I had to die. I had to experience the death of the old life, the sinful life, the life where I was in control, a life where I was the center. This surrendering of ourselves is so foreign to our human nature, a nature that fights against

God tooth and nail. But God, by His mercy, can quicken the dead to life through the power of His Holy Spirit.

My whole life turned upside down—or should I say right side up. I had been changed from the inside. My sinful desires to be with the other woman vanished. All my unsuccessful attempts at trying to do this through my own willpower were in vain. I was captive to the power of my sinful nature. I was blind to the truth. God's righteous Son now lives with me in my heart. It is He that I now live through. It is because of Him that I can now call God my Father, and it is through Him that I can now please the Father. I was given a new set of eyes and a heart of flesh that replaced my heart of stone.

Suddenly, I was filled with an insatiable appetite for the things of God. This was the work of God Himself starting His process of restoration in me through the work of His Holy Spirit. He implanted into my heart the desire for things that I never desired before. For example, I had never picked up a Bible before in my life to read. I just did not have the desire. But now I wanted to read it. I wanted to know more about God. In fact, I couldn't seem to get enough of it.

My love for my wife was restored. God had miraculously healed our marriage. By the power and grace of God, never again would I sin against my wife and children in such a way. God had taken away the sinful, powerful desires of adultery. When you are forgiven much, you love much. I wanted to know more and more about the God of the Bible.

I couldn't sleep at night, I had so many questions flying through my mind. My old life had ended; a new life had begun. For the first time in my life I had truly experienced the forgiveness of God. I had now come to realize that I couldn't make myself righteous before God. This, in fact, is the very reason that Jesus went to the cross and suffered His death. He was paying the price for my sin. He is the One who is the narrow path to heaven. It is *in Him* that I must rest. It is *in Him, and Him alone,* that I need to place my trust for my rescue.

I had believed that if a person followed the Law and the commandments that one could be found righteous by God. But I didn't understand that the Law couldn't save. The Bible teaches that not only can the Law not save us, but in fact it actually condemns us! We do not realize this truth because we are dead in our sins; we are deceived by our sins.

I did not understand that God declares us right through our faith in Him, not by our works. It is God who makes us right with Him, by our faith in His Son, His only Son. We are made alive by the Spirit; it is He who gives us life. The Spirit enables us to love and serve our Lord. We are dependent upon God's mercy to rescue us from our own darkness. Only Christ is more powerful than sin. It is He who has conquered death by His resurrection.

We need to rest in *His* work. When we try to save ourselves, we end up forfeiting our soul. In essence, we nullify the work of our One true Redeemer. We must trust in the work of Jesus on the cross. He has come to save us. Our faith must be centered and rooted in *Him,* not in a religious system. It is by God's grace that we find new life. It is His gift. We can't obligate God for this gift.

Listen to what the apostle Paul said to a group of people who thought they could earn their righteousness before God by trying to keep the laws. Paul told them, "I do not set aside the grace of God, for if righteousness could be gained through the law, Christ died for nothing!" (Galatians 2:21). But Christ did not die for nothing. He died for you and for me. He died to completely pay for the punishment due to our personal sins. This is the person we need to surrender our lives to! This is the person we are to trust for eternal life.

As I reflect back on my life, I think of my inner beliefs before I experienced God personally. I would certainly say that I believed in the existence of God. I believed in the laws of God, and I believed that we were to obey the commandments. I believed in the Catholic Church as the only true Church. The Church had taught me all that I knew about God. I sincerely believed that if I had unconfessed mortal sin on my soul when I died, that it would condemn me to hell. I believed that the only way to receive forgiveness for sins was to confess them to a duly authorized priest. I believed that my good works would help me to find favor with God come judgment day. I believed that all these things contributed toward attaining my personal salvation.

But as I look back on those years of trying to find happiness, I find that God was at work putting many people in my path to draw sketches for me of God. For I lived in a cave, the darkness of my sinful nature. God had allowed me, by following the pathway of sin, to discover that He is the only One who can overcome the power of my sin. God allowed me to experience the depravity of my inner being and my inability to save myself.

The sketches of a God who loves us first, even though God is not shown love, were drawn for me by my wife, Noreen, in her deep love for me. The sketch of a God who yearns for us through the petitioning of prayers was drawn for me by my beloved mother before her death, my faithful sister Susan Miller, my former pastor Rev. Rich Plass, my sister-in-law Jody, and many others. And finally God used the evangelist, Rev. John Guest, to draw the sketch of God, who gave us His one and only Son to suffer and die for us, as he faithfully preached the Gospel through his brilliant story that Friday morning. God used His faithful saints to make Himself known to a man who lived in a cave. This is a beautiful picture of God reaching out to man.

You may be fearful of standing before God. You may be petrified of your own death. Your life may be filled with people, material things, and maybe even church, but deep in your heart you have emptiness that you keep trying to fill. A silent void in your life is deafening.

Your life may be much like mine; you grew up with a basic understanding of God and His kingdom. You believe in God, maybe always have, but something's not right, something's missing. You are trying to live a decent life, a moral life. You try to obey all the commandments of God and the Church, but you can't seem to keep them all at any one time. You are fearful that you may come up short of God's standards. Or worse yet, you may not know what standards God actually will use.

You might be trying to fill your life with things that will bring joy and peace. You look for that fulfillment and satisfaction through your children or your spouse or your job. You may be seeking wealth, or possibly power and prestige. You may, in fact, even say you have tried to become more religious, but it doesn't seem to satisfy. Religion as an end never works. In fact Jesus Himself had more confrontations with religious leaders than with any other group.

It is not any religion that gives true life; it is a person, the person of God. But there is good news, and the good news is this: You can know the happiness, peace, and joy you are seeking. The good news is—you can know it even now! But obviously it is not I who can give peace to you; I can only put your hand on the door. Through the writings of this book, I can only draw you a sketch. You yourself must experience God. You yourself must decide whether to rely on your own best efforts or to trust God's own answer for your sin.

Chapter Seventeen

"IT IS FINISHED"

David was a very young boy who volunteered to fight a large, strong Philistine man who was a great warrior. All of the adult men shuddered at the thought of potential combat with the warrior, Goliath. Here's the picture—you have one giant sized he-man, equipped with a sword that could easily rip a human body to shreds. And you have one small, young boy, who by training is not a soldier, but rather a sheepherder. The boy is not equipped with a sword but instead a small slingshot, hardly a match for the mighty sword. In this story we have the weak taking on the powerful.

You likely know the ending. David the shepherd boy defeats Goliath the warrior-man with a well-placed shot to the forehead from his sling. The weak overcomes the powerful. By human standards, David was not equipped in the least to win. By all logic he should have perished under the mighty sword-wielding warrior named Goliath. But the truth is that he was saved from physical death.

Why did he survive? you may ask. Because David

brought one powerful weapon with him into the battle-field: his faith in his Savior. David said, "You come against me with sword and spear and javelin, but I come against you in the name of the Lord Almighty" (1 Samuel 17:45). He looked death squarely in the face and challenged his mighty opponent with only one weapon: He was walking in the name of God. David was sincere in believing that his God was with him. He trusted that his God would save him. His faith was so simple, yet so powerful. The grace of God was with David, and David's faith was with God. They go hand in hand: grace by the Creator and faith by the creation.

Life is like the battle of David and Goliath. It is the powerful against the weak. Whether we realize it or not, we too must battle a mighty warrior. His name, however, is not Goliath; it is Death. This battle is not only for our physical body, but also more importantly for our spiritu-al soul. It is a battle that we all engage in. Yet we shake in our boots at the thought of fighting such a powerful enemy. How can we stand against such a threatening foe?

There is only one way, but it is a way that many ridicule and scorn—a way that, to many, appears impos-sible or even foolish. A way that defies human logic. A way that is beyond the comprehension of even the most intelligent military strategist!

If we are to survive the threat, we must enter the bat-tlefield with someone who is stronger than Goliath. Someone who has defeated death itself. Someone who has already fought the strongman and has won. Unfortu-nately, due to unbelief, pride, and arrogance among the combatants, the strongman will defeat many. Only a few find the One who can redeem us from the clutches of death. It seems only a few are willing to believe that we cannot defeat the strongman on our own. We keep seeking stronger weapons, more intelligence, and more self-reliance.

David won the battle with Goliath. Why? Pure and simple, because God was with him. It wasn't his weapon, it wasn't his bravery, it wasn't his keen sense of shot. It was God who put down the strongman Goliath. It was because of God's mercy on David that he won the battle. God's mercy was manifested to David through his faith in God. David believed with his whole heart and soul that God would rescue him from death. David's faith rested in the power of God Almighty; he did not rest in his own power and skills.

David experienced God!

If you can grasp the significance of this story, you have been given the keys to unlock the door that leads to life.

If you and I try to face the strongman by ourselves, we will ultimately be defeated. We will lose the battle that faces each of us. Our destiny will be an eternal death, a separation from God forever. Sister Malvina's words will ring true, "Always be in; never get out."

But like David, we need to trust in the One who has already won the victory over death. We need to trust in Jesus, who won our battle for us against the power and destruction of our sin. Just before Jesus died on the cross, He uttered three famous words that speak volumes. He said, "It is finished" (John 19:30).

In other words, the price was now completely paid. The Father's wrath for sin was delivered to His Son. The holiness of God was preserved on the cross at Calvary. The battle victory was secured, the strongman was defeated on the cross by the Man who others mocked as weak. The perfect One sacrificed His life for His enemies. He took the sword in His side so that we may live, so that we can be set free from death.

When we hit the battlefield against sin in our life, we must rely on the grace of God to save us. To rely on ourselves or others will surely bring defeat. Instead we take with us our faith in Christ's work on the cross, the helmet of our salvation. We take with us our faith in His resurrection from the dead, the shield from death. We take with us His promise of eternal life to all those who believe in Him. *Our weapon is a shield, our faith*—our faith in the person of Jesus Christ and Jesus alone!

I wrote this book for one purpose, so that you may know Jesus. So that you may know the peace that is beyond all understanding and the true hope that only God can give. My desire for you is echoed by the words of the apostle Paul when he said to the Romans, "May the God of hope fill you with all joy and peace *as you trust in him,* so that you may overflow with hope by the power of the Holy Spirit" (Romans 15:13, italics added).

Dear friends, this is where my story ends. My hope is that it is only the beginning for you. Remember, the beginning of true life is found on your knees.

If you sense God making Himself known to you, please read the following prayer with a sincere and trusting heart:

In the name of the Father, and the Son, and the Holy Spirit—dearest God, I come before You now with a humble heart that I realize is far from You. I want to ask for Your forgiveness for all of my sins. I realize there is nothing I can do toward my own salvation. I want to have new life in Your Son Jesus, Your one and only Son who gave His life as a sacrifice to You for my transgressions.

I give my life into Your hands. I am trusting that Your Son is the truth and the way to You. Please renew my life, through Your Holy Spirit, and fill my heart with Your desires. I ask You right now for this new life that only You can give. May You make known to me Your wonderful love and forgiveness and grant me peace with You. Amen.

"Now to him who is able to establish you by my gospel and the proclamation of Jesus Christ, . . . to the only wise God be glory forever through Jesus Christ! Amen" (Romans 16:25, 27).

If you are interested in information
about other books written from a
biblical perspective, please write
to the following address:

Northfield Publishing
215 West Locust Street
Chicago, IL 60610